150 GREAT AMERICANS

WILLIAM J. BENNETT AND JOHN T. E. CRIBB

NELSON
BOOKS

An Imprint of Thomas Nelson

150 Great Americans

© 2022 William J. Bennett and John T. E. Cribb

Portions of this book were adapted from *The American Patriot's Almanac*
(ISBN 978-1-5955-5267-9) © 2010.

Published in Nashville, Tennessee, by Nelson Books, an imprint of Thomas Nelson. Nelson Books and Thomas Nelson are registered trademarks of HarperCollins Christian Publishing, Inc.

Thomas Nelson titles may be purchased in bulk for educational, business, fundraising, or sales promotional use. For information, please email SpecialMarkets@ ThomasNelson.com.

ISBN 978-1-4003-2579-5
ISBN 978-1-4003-2612-9 (audiobook)
ISBN 978-1-4003-2603-7 (eBook)

Library of Congress Cataloging-in-Publication Data on File

Printed in the United States

22 23 24 25 26 LSC 5 4 3 2 1

*I*n 1838, when Abraham Lincoln was a young man, he gave a speech in Springfield, Illinois, in which he shared his thoughts on the fabric of our nation. He observed that America's founding generation had passed away. He believed people like George Washington and Thomas Jefferson had been pillars of the temple of liberty. "Now that they have crumbled away, that temple must fall," Lincoln said, "unless we, their descendants, supply their places with other pillars."

What should those new pillars be? Lincoln's answer: "general intelligence," "sound morality," and "a reverence for the Constitution and laws" among the American people.

By "general intelligence," he meant the knowledge and skills people need to be responsible citizens. Lincoln knew that the health of democracy depends on individuals making intelligent decisions, not just on election day, but in their daily lives.

By "sound morality," Lincoln was talking about good character. He knew the character of the nation depends on the character of its citizens and how they conduct themselves.

By "a reverence for the Constitution and laws," Lincoln was referring to good civics education and respect for basic institutions. "Let reverence for the laws be breathed by every American mother to the lisping babe that prattles on her lap—let it be taught in schools, in seminaries, and in colleges," he said.

All these things come, in part, by knowing some history, particularly the events and people that make up our country's past—the kind of stories you find in this book.

The long winter at Valley Forge. Susan B. Anthony's vote and trial.

The Wright Brothers at Kitty Hawk. The Reverend Martin Luther King Jr.'s "I Have a Dream" speech.

Knowing such history helps us understand the world around us. It helps us understand our duties to neighbors and country.

Our history is a heritage we Americans all share. It ties us together, like a common language or currency. Knowing that heritage helps us understand the central principles underlying American democracy and our responsibilities in passing them on to the next generation.

Perhaps most important, knowing the stories in this book helps us love our country. It helps us become patriots. After all, you have to know something before you can really love it.

America badly needs patriotism informed by a solid knowledge of our country and its past. At a time when so many seem to be losing sight of our identity as a nation, it is more important than ever to remember our heritage, not only so we can know who we are today, but to set us on the right path for the future.

After he was elected president, Lincoln spoke to the American people of "the mystic chords of memory stretching from every battlefield and patriot grave to every living heart and hearthstone all over this broad land."

The people and events in these pages, including Lincoln himself, are all part of those "mystic chords." We hope this book helps connect you and your family to those chords and to this great nation's heritage.

William J. Bennett and John Cribb

CONTENTS

Foreword iii

In Search of the Fountain of Youth. 1

Pocahontas. 3

The Fortitude of Our Forefathers 5

The National Guard 6

Anne Hutchinson 7

Harvard Gets a Name. 8

Marquette Explores the Heart of the Continent. 9

William Penn. 11

George Washington 12

John Peter Zenger 13

Proverbs from *Poor Richard's Almanack*. 14

Mary Draper Ingles. 16

Daniel Boone in Kentucky. 18

Always Go Forward. 20

Phillis Wheatley 22

Israel Putnam 24

Mount Vernon 26

The US Army Origins and Flag. 28

Abigail Adams. 29

The Navy Birthday and Flag 30

The Marine Corps Birthday and Flag 31

Thomas Paine Publishes *Common Sense* 32

Henry Knox's Long Haul 34

Betsy Ross. 36

John Witherspoon, Parson and Patriot 37

Caesar Rodney's Ride 39

John Hancock. 40

They Risked All 41

But One Life to Lose 43

The Times That Try Men's Souls 44

Haym Salomon: A Financial Hero of the Revolution. 45

Lafayette and the Sentry 47

Molly Pitcher 48

Not Yet Begun 49

Jane Thomas's Ride. 50

Benedict Arnold Commits Treason 51

The Swamp Fox 53

A Devil of a Whipping 54

The President with Shoot in His Eyes 55

The Patriot Who Burned Her Home 57

Jack Jouett's Ride. 58

James Forten, Freedom Fighter. 60

Betty Zane 62

What Is an American? 64

The Father of the Constitution 65

Alexander Hamilton. 67

Martha Washington 68

The Coast Guard Birthday and Flag. 69

Benjamin Banneker 70

Abigail Adams. 72

First in the Hearts. 74

Johnny Appleseed 76

Sacagawea. 77

Fulton's Folly 78

Elizabeth Ann Seton. 79

Don't Give Up. 80

Dolley Madison 81

The Santa Fe Trail 82

James Monroe 83

The Ways of Providence. 84

Praise of Liberty 85

Frederick Douglass 86

Lincoln's Bumpy Road 87

Old Man Eloquent and the *Amistad* 88

Presidential Trivia. 90

Samuel Morse Starts a Communications Revolution 92

The Donner Party 94

Elizabeth Blackwell. 96

A Woman Called Moses. 98

We Are All Descendants of 1776. 99

Sam Houston 101

The Battle Hymn of the Republic 102

Your Soldier Boy 103

Lee at Gettysburg 104

Mary Edwards Walker 105

Full Speed Ahead. 106

Jane Addams 107

John Wesley Powell: Into the Unknown 109

Susan B. Anthony 111

Buffalo Bill. 112

Annie Oakley. 113

Mr. Watson, Come Here. 114

Laura Ingalls Wilder. 115

The Greatest Inventor of Them All. 116

Angel of the Battlefield. 118

Grant's Memoirs 119

A Daring Adventure 121

Around the World in Seventy-Two Days 123

Mark Twain on Foreign Critics. 125

The Origins of Basketball 127

Presidential Trivia. 128

The Man Who Gave Back. 130

The Man in the Arena 131

The President and the Teddy Bear 132

A Few Presidential Firsts 133

A Horseless Carriage. 135

The US Military Reserve 136

Mottos and Watchwords of Some Who Defend Us 137

The Birth of the FBI 138

A Citizen of the World 140

America's First Lady of the Air 141

Uncle Sam. 143

One Hero's Pledge 144

Eddie Rickenbacker, Ace of Aces 145

Sergeant York. 147

The American Legion. 148

Mary McLeod Bethune. 149

Fear Itself 150

The Father of Modern Rocketry 151

The Spirit of St. Louis. 153

Philo Farnsworth, the Forgotten Inventor 154

Jesse Owens at Berlin 156

Disney's Follies 157

Amelia Earhart's Last Flight 158

Eleanor Roosevelt 159

The Iron Horse. 160

FDR's "Day of Infamy" Address 162

Bob Hope, Honorary Veteran 164

I Shall Return. 166

Butch O'Hare Saves the *Lexington* 167

The Navajo Code Talkers 169

Rosie the Riveter 170

The Four Chaplains 171

The Tuskegee Airmen. 172

The Jefferson Memorial 173

PT-109. 175

If Any Blame 176

The Pied Piper of Saipan 177

The Youngest Pilot in the Navy. 178

Audie Murphy 180

The Buck Stops Here. 181

The Air Force Birthday and Flag 182

Chuck Yeager 183

Give 'Em Hell, Harry 184

Elvis Hits the Airwaves 185

Born in the USA. 186

Remembering Martin Luther King Jr.. 188

The Freedom Riders 190

Godspeed, John Glenn 191

No Shortage of Heroes 193

The POW/MIA Flag 194

One of Hollywood's Finest. 195

Keep Swinging. 197

Presidential Trivia. 198

The Bible and the Oath. 200

Forgot to Duck. 201

Ronald Reagan. 202

Honorary Citizens of the United States 203

Home Alive. 205

Pat Tillman's Sacrifice 207

IN SEARCH OF THE FOUNTAIN OF YOUTH

*F*loridians observe April 2 as Pascua Florida Day, the day in 1513 that Spanish adventurer Juan Ponce de León made the first known landing in Florida by a European explorer.

Ponce de León, born to a noble family in Spain, first came to the New World in 1493 with Christopher Columbus's second expedition. He later conquered Puerto Rico and became its first governor. According to tradition, it was there that the Indians told him of an island to the west blessed with not only gold but a magical spring that restored youth and cured illnesses.

In 1513 the eager conquistador sailed from Puerto Rico with three ships to find the island, its gold, and its miraculous fountain. On April 2 he stepped onto a beach somewhere near present-day St. Augustine (the exact spot is uncertain) and claimed the land for Spain. He named it "Florida" because he arrived at Easter time, which the Spaniards called Pascua Florida, the Feast of the Flowers.

The Spaniards sailed around the southern end of Florida, which they still took to be a giant island, and up the west coast. Finding neither gold nor the mysterious fountain of youth, they returned to Puerto Rico.

Eight years later, Ponce de León made a second trip to Florida, this time determined to found a settlement. He landed on the west coast with some two hundred men, horses, cattle, and supplies, but the Spaniards soon found themselves at war with Calusa Indians who shot poison arrows. One of the arrows struck Ponce de León, and the entire expedition fled for Cuba, where the tough old conquistador soon died. He was buried in Puerto Rico, the words "Here rest the bones of a lion" inscribed on his tomb. So ended the legendary search for the fountain of youth.

POCAHONTAS

*M*uch legend surrounds the life of Pocahontas, but the known facts are remarkable enough. Born around the year 1595 to Powhatan, chief of a powerful tribe, she was about twelve years old when English colonists founded Jamestown, Virginia. According to Captain John Smith, it was Pocahontas who saved him when the Indians took him prisoner. Just as the executioners were about to bash in his head, Smith wrote, Pocahontas "got his head in her armes, and laid her owne upon his to save him from death."

Some scholars have suggested that what Smith took to be an "execution" was really a ceremony of some kind. At any rate Powhatan set Smith free, and young Pocahontas became a frequent visitor to Jamestown, sometimes bringing food to the hungry settlers. Her friendly nature (her name means "playful one") made her a favorite among the colonists.

A few years later, after Smith left for England, the settlers kidnapped the Indian maiden, intending to hold her until her father returned some prisoners and stolen supplies. During her captivity, Pocahontas converted to Christianity and was baptized as Rebecca. With her father's consent, she married colonist John Rolfe, and the couple had a boy, Thomas. The marriage helped bring peace between the Indians and settlers.

In 1616 the Rolfes sailed to England to help promote the Jamestown colony. There the Indian "princess" was treated as a celebrity and welcomed at royal festivities. But she grew ill and died just before she was to return to Virginia. She was buried on March 21, 1617, in the town of Gravesend.

Pocahontas's story has been told a hundred ways in books, poems, plays, and movies. She was undoubtedly a courageous young woman who tried to bring friendship between two peoples. Captain Smith may have left the best tribute when he said she was "the instrument to [preserve] this colonie from death, famine, and utter confusion."

THE FORTITUDE OF
OUR FOREFATHERS

*O*n December 21, 1620, the first landing party of Pilgrims came ashore in Massachusetts at the place they named Plymouth. There they founded the second successful English settlement in America. (The first was Jamestown, Virginia.) Tradition says that as they came ashore, the Pilgrims set foot on a granite boulder called Plymouth Rock, now a famous symbol of resolution and faith.

Nearly a century and a half later, in his *Dissertation on the Canon and Feudal Law*, John Adams of Massachusetts urged his countrymen not to forget the trials the early American colonists faced and the reasons they came to America:

> Let us read and recollect and impress upon our souls the views and ends of our . . . forefathers, in exchanging their native country for a dreary, inhospitable wilderness. . . . Recollect their amazing fortitude, their bitter sufferings—the hunger, the nakedness, the cold, which they patiently endured—the severe labors of clearing their grounds, building their houses, raising their provisions, amidst dangers from wild beasts and savage men, before they had time or money or materials for commerce. Recollect the civil and religious principles and hopes and expectations which constantly supported and carried them through all hardships with patience and resignation. Let us recollect it was liberty, the hope of liberty, for themselves and us and ours, which conquered all discouragements, dangers, and trials.

THE NATIONAL GUARD

*T*he National Guard is the oldest part of our nation's armed forces, tracing its roots to the time when the thirteen original English colonies required able-bodied male citizens to train and be ready to defend their communities. The Guard observes December 13 as its birthday because on that day in 1636, the Massachusetts Bay Colony organized scattered militia companies from villages around Boston into three regiments. Articles I and II of the US Constitution lay down guidelines providing for the National Guard.

Today's Guard is made of men and women—businessmen, factory workers, teachers, doctors, police officers—who volunteer on a part-time basis. Each state and territory, as well as the District of Columbia, has its own National Guard. Army National Guard units are part of the US Army. Air National Guard units are part of the US Air Force.

Guard members have a unique dual mission that requires them to swear an oath of allegiance to their state and to the federal government. In times of peace, the governor of each state commands its National Guard and can call it into action if needed. Guard members stand ready to natural disasters and other crises.

The second part of the Guard's job is to defend America and respond to national emergencies. During times of war or national need, the president can call up the National Guard. In wartime Guard members constitute a large portion of the US fighting force. Guard personnel pour much time and energy into training. Units take part in efforts ranging from blood drives to the fight against terrorism. The motto of these citizen soldiers is "Always ready, always there."

ANNE HUTCHINSON

*Y*our opinions frett like a Gangrene and spread like a Leprosie." Such were the criticisms that authorities in the Massachusetts Bay Colony leveled at Anne Hutchinson.

Hutchinson came to Boston with her husband and children in 1634, serving as a midwife. She invited neighbors into her home to discuss sermons and study the Bible. Being well versed in theology, the meetings attracted a steady following.

Soon Anne's commentaries roused the ire of John Winthrop, longtime Puritan leader. Winthrop considered some of her teachings, such as that people could communicate with God directly without the aid of church officials, a threat to his "city upon a hill." He did not like the idea of an outspoken woman challenging Puritan authorities.

What began as a quarrel over religious doctrine turned into a struggle for influence. Hutchinson was brought to trial and accused of betraying the laws of church and state. She retorted that Winthrop's edicts were "for those who have not the light which makes plain the pathway"—she didn't need colonial officials to tell her how to practice her faith.

Hutchinson refused to yield, and on March 22, 1638, she was banished from the colony. She moved with her family and several followers to Rhode Island, where she helped found Portsmouth. She later moved to New York where, in 1643, she was killed in an Indian attack.

Today Anne Hutchinson is remembered as a pioneer who stood up for some freedoms now embedded in our Constitution. The inscription on her statue in front of Boston's State House reads, in part: "In Memory of Anne Marbury Hutchinson . . . Courageous Exponent of Civil Liberty and Religious Toleration."

HARVARD GETS A NAME

O n March 13, 1639, the oldest institution of higher learning in the United States was named for Puritan minister John Harvard, one of the school's earliest and greatest benefactors. John Harvard was born in 1607 near the Surrey end of London Bridge, and as a young man he received his education at the University of Cambridge. By the 1630s, his father and most of his family had died of the plague. His inheritance made him a well-to-do member of England's middle class.

Faced with religious persecution, Harvard joined the wave of Puritans emigrating to America for a better life and chance to worship freely. In 1637 he and his wife, Ann, arrived in New England and became inhabitants of Charlestown, Massachusetts. That same year, he became a teaching elder of the First Church of Charlestown, a position that required him to explain Scripture and give sermons.

But John Harvard did not last long in the New World. A little more than a year after his arrival, he died of consumption. On his deathbed he bequeathed 779 pounds (half his estate) and a collection of about four hundred books to a college that had been founded in 1636 in Newtown (now Cambridge, Massachusetts).

It was a generous gift, one that helped launch the fledgling college on its mission to educate students in a classical curriculum and Puritan theology. In 1639 the Massachusetts General Court decided to name the school Harvard College in honor of the minister. Today the name Harvard is a good reminder that many of this country's finest universities trace their roots to churches and clergymen who realized that without educated citizens, America could not thrive.

MARQUETTE EXPLORES THE HEART OF THE CONTINENT

*T*he Indians spoke of a great river to the south, a "father of waters" that flowed all the way to the sea. Jacques Marquette, a Jesuit missionary from France, was determined to find the mysterious waterway. Perhaps it was the long-sought route to the Pacific. In the spring of 1673, he left northern Michigan with fur trader Louis Jolliet and five others in two canoes. In mid-June, the explorers shot down the Wisconsin River and reached the Mississippi.

They floated south through lands no Europeans had visited before, stopping to smoke the peace pipe with Indians they met. They passed the thundering mouth of the Missouri River in full flood and heard reports that it led to a western sea (reports that Lewis and Clark would later test). Buffalo with heads "a foot and a half wide between the horns" roamed the prairies. Marquette recorded that "from time to time we came upon monstrous fish, one of which struck our canoe with such violence that I thought that it was a great tree about to break the canoe to pieces."

They traveled 1,700 miles to the mouth of the Arkansas River. By that time, they realized the Mississippi must drain into the Gulf of Mexico, rather than the Pacific. Wary of being captured by Spaniards, they turned and headed home.

The next year, Marquette set out to found a mission among the Illinois Indians. On December 4, 1674, he and two companions became the first white men to build a dwelling at a site that would someday become Chicago. But the intrepid priest grew ill, his strength failed, and he died in 1675 near Ludington, Michigan.

Father Jacques Marquette never discovered the fabled route to the western sea. But his explorations turned vague rumors into known facts, and helped open the way to America's heartland.

WILLIAM PENN

$\mathcal{W}$illiam Penn was a constant source of frustration for his father, a wealthy English admiral. The rebellious younger Penn got kicked out of Oxford University for refusing to attend Anglican (Church of England) services. Then he joined the Society of Friends, a religious sect known as the Quakers because their leader had once told an English judge to "tremble at the Word of the Lord." Quakers' religious beliefs and refusal to swear allegiance to any king but God led to their persecution. William Penn found himself imprisoned more than once.

Admiral Penn was an old friend of King Charles II and loaned the monarch a good deal of money. When the admiral died, William asked that the debt be paid with land in America. The king liked William, despite his religious beliefs, and granted him a huge tract of wilderness, which Charles named Pennsylvania, meaning "Penn's woods."

On August 30, 1682, William Penn sailed for America to begin his "Holy Experiment"—a colony that would be a refuge for not only Quakers but settlers of various faiths. Penn's guarantee of religious freedom was then one of the most comprehensive in the world. Indeed, his plan to include diverse populations while extending a broad measure of religious and political equality was nothing less than revolutionary for its time.

Catholics, Lutherans, Baptists, Presbyterians, French Huguenots, and even Anglicans rushed to settle the rich lands. By 1700, Pennsylvania had as many as 21,000 settlers. The capital, Philadelphia ("City of Brotherly Love"), became a thriving metropolis, soon the largest of North America's colonial cities. As settlers arrived—English, Scots-Irish, Welsh, German, Dutch, Swedish, and more—Penn's woods began to resemble the famous American "melting pot."

GEORGE WASHINGTON

*G*eorge Washington was born on February 22, 1732, in Westmoreland County, in eastern Virginia. In three crucial ways he shaped our nation. First, he led American forces during the fight for independence. Second, he presided over the writing of our Constitution. Third, he served as our first president.

At times, it was Washington's character alone that seemed to hold the fledgling United States together. He became a symbol of what Americans were struggling for, risking his life and fortune to lead his countrymen to liberty.

During one battle of the Revolution, at Monmouth in New Jersey, the American troops were in confused flight and on the verge of destruction when General Washington appeared on the field. Soldiers stopped in their tracks and stared as the tall, blue-coated figure spurred his horse up and down the line, halting the retreat. The young Marquis de Lafayette remembered the sight for the rest of his life, how Washington rode "all along the lines amid the shouts of the soldiers, cheering them by his voice and example and restoring to our standard the fortunes of the fight. I thought then, as now, that never had I beheld so superb a man."

The general turned his army around. The fighting raged until sundown, and that night the British took the chance to slip away. Washington's very presence had stopped a rout and turned the tide of battle.

It was not the only time. Again and again, Americans turned to Washington. He was, as biographer James Flexner called him, the "indispensable man" of the American founding.

Without George Washington, there may never have been a United States.

JOHN PETER ZENGER

*W*illiam Cosby, England's governor for the colony of New York, was a bully and a scoundrel. He tried to silence opponents, rig elections, and use his office to make himself rich. But Cosby had a problem: John Peter Zenger and his printing press. Zenger, a German immigrant, began publishing his *New York Weekly Journal* in 1733, and he made it his business to publicize Cosby's greed and arrogance.

Cosby reacted by sending his henchmen to seize and burn copies of the paper. Zenger went right on printing. In 1734 the governor tried to silence Zenger for good by having him arrested for seditious libel. At Cosby's request, bail was set much higher than Zenger could pay. For nearly nine months he sat in prison while his wife, Anna, helped publish the paper.

Finally Zenger got his day in court. But the governor's handpicked judges disbarred his lawyers, leaving him without counsel. Andrew Hamilton, one of the finest attorneys in the colonies, rose from his sickbed in Philadelphia and journeyed to New York City to defend the printer.

The court all but ordered the jurors to find Zenger guilty of libel. Hamilton reminded them that the printer's only crime was that he had dared to publish the truth. It did not take long for the jury to reach a decision. On August 4, 1735, it returned its verdict: not guilty.

The trial set a precedent for America's world-famous freedom of the press. Journalists sometimes abuse that freedom in pursuit of their own agendas. Still, the First Amendment remains an American bedrock. As Zenger's newspaper put it, "No nation ancient or modern has ever lost the liberty of freely speaking, writing or publishing their sentiments, but forthwith lost their liberty in general and became slaves."

PROVERBS FROM *POOR RICHARD'S ALMANACK*

*M*any American colonists started each year by opening the latest edition of their favorite almanac. The most famous was *Poor Richard's Almanack*, published by Benjamin Franklin from 1733 to 1758, while he was a printer in Philadelphia. Readers appreciated the almanac's weather predictions, astronomical data, and agricultural information. But they especially loved its humor, verses, and practical advice, all dispensed by the pen of "Poor" Richard Saunders, a fictional astrologer whom Franklin invented to be the editor of his publication.

Some of Poor Richard's proverbs—such as "A penny saved is a penny earned" and "Early to bed and early to rise, makes a man healthy, wealthy, and wise"—are still quoted today. Many of the aphorisms came from earlier writers, ranging from Greek to English, but were often "Americanized" for Franklin's readers.

A few more proverbs from Poor Richard:

- With the old Almanack and the old year Leave thy old vices, tho'ever so dear.
- He that riseth late must trot all day, and shall scarce overtake his business at night.
- Well done is better than well said.
- People who are wrapped up in themselves make small packages.
- Little strokes fell great oaks.

- If a man could have half his wishes, he would double his troubles.
- One today is worth two tomorrows.
- He that by the plow would thrive, Himself must either hold or drive.
- Laziness travels so slowly that Poverty soon overtakes him.

MARY DRAPER INGLES

*T*he story of Mary Draper Ingles is a good reminder of the harsh and sometimes brutal conditions that early settlers faced.

On July 30 or 31, 1755 (the exact date is uncertain), a band of Shawnee Indians swooped down on a frontier settlement called Draper's Meadow in what is now Blacksburg, Virginia, killing four people and capturing several more. Among the hostages were twenty-three-year-old Mary Draper Ingles and her two sons, four-year-old Thomas and two-year-old George. Mary's husband, William, who had been in a field, harvesting wheat, avoided capture.

The Shawnee headed northwest, forcing their captives over the Appalachian Mountains. According to one account, Mary was pregnant and soon gave birth to a daughter, who may have died on the trail. Other reports make no mention of a baby. At any rate, the Shawnee led their captives to a village on the Ohio River. There Mary was separated from her sons. She and another captive described as "the Old Dutch Woman" were taken farther north to Big Bone Lick, near present-day Cincinnati, where they were put to work making salt.

One October afternoon, the two white women slipped into the forest and set off on an eight-hundred-mile-long escape. Avoiding trails for fear of recapture, they backtracked over the mountains, scaling cliffs in places, living on walnuts and wild grapes as they fled. Winter arrived. They trudged through snow and slept in hollow logs. Half mad from exhaustion and hunger, the Old Dutch Woman tried to kill Mary, who managed to get away.

Six weeks after escaping the Indians, a skeletal, ragged Mary Draper Ingles staggered into a cornfield near her old home. She soon reunited with her husband, who had gone to Tennessee and Georgia looking for her. They resumed their pioneer lives and went on to have four more children. Mary lived until 1815, dying at age eighty-three.

DANIEL BOONE IN KENTUCKY

*I*n 1769 Daniel Boone made camp among the rolling, forested hills of a hunter's paradise he had long dreamed of exploring. He had spent several weeks trekking over the Appalachian Mountains, having "resigned my domestic happiness for a time, and left my family and peaceable habitation on the Yadkin River in North Carolina, to wander through the wilderness of America, in quest of the country of Kentucke." He later recalled his arrival:

We proceeded successfully, and after a long and fatiguing journey through a mountainous wilderness, in a westward direction, on the seventh day of June following, we found ourselves on Red River . . . and, from the top of an eminence, saw with pleasure the beautiful level of Kentucke. . . . At this place we encamped, and made a shelter to defend us from the inclement season, and began to hunt and reconnoitre the country. We found everywhere abundance of wild beasts of all sorts, through this vast forest. The buffaloes were more frequent than I have seen cattle in the settlements, browzing on the leaves of the cane, or cropping the herbage on those extensive plains, fearless, because igno-rant, of the violence of man. Sometimes we saw hundreds in a drove, and the numbers about the salt springs were amazing. In this forest, the habitation of beasts of every kind natural to America, we practised hunting with great success until the twenty-second day of December following.

Boone was already becoming a legendary explorer. ("I can't say as ever I was lost, but I was bewildered once for three days," he said.) In 1775 he blazed the Wilderness Road through Cumberland Gap, establishing a main westward route through the Appalachians. Thousands of tough, resourceful pioneers followed him into the wild, fertile land of Kentucky and beyond.

ALWAYS GO FORWARD

*D*ay by day this country seems to grow bigger and bigger with great walls and fortress-like bastions rising up to defend the west coast. They force us to make many detours, thus more than doubling the length of our march."

So wrote Franciscan friar Junipero Serra in the summer of 1769 as he limped north through the desert with a Spanish expedition headed from Mexico to San Diego Bay. The fifty-six-year-old Serra, a native of the Spanish island of Majorca, had been given the task of starting the first mission in what is now California.

He was not in the best condition for trail blazing. An infection caused by an insect bite had left one of his legs permanently injured. "When I saw him with his swollen foot and leg with its ulcer, I could not keep back the tears," recalled another padre who saw him begin the trek. The soldiers in the expedition urged Serra to return to Mexico. The friar, who had adopted the motto "Always go forward and never turn back," refused.

At one point, his foot grew so inflamed, he could not walk. He asked the young man who took care of the mules to make a poultice. "But father, I only know how to treat sores on mules," the man protested. "Then pretend I am a mule," Serra replied, and the muleteer applied an ointment.

On July 1, 1769, the expedition rendezvoused with two ships at San Diego Bay and began building a settlement at what is now the city of

San Diego. On July 16, Serra founded Mission San Diego de Alcalá when he raised a wooden cross and sang a mass. The tireless friar spent the remaining fifteen years of his life limping hundreds of miles up and down the coast, founding a string of missions that became the first major European effort to settle California.

PHILLIS WHEATLEY

September 1, 1773, saw the publication of Phillis Wheatley's *Poems on Various Subjects, Religious and Moral*, the first volume of poetry by an African American poet.

Born in Senegal, West Africa, Phillis Wheatley was sold into slavery around age seven, taken to Boston, and purchased off a slave ship by John Wheatley, a wealthy merchant. The Wheatley family taught her to read and write, and by age fourteen she began composing poetry. Most Bostonians found it hard to believe that a young slave girl could produce such lyrics, but a group of the city's most notable citizens, including John Hancock, gave her an oral examination and signed a letter "To the Publick" attesting to her authorship.

No Boston publisher would print her work, so admirers arranged for publication in London. Freed by the Wheatleys, Phillis sailed for a visit to England, where the Lord Mayor of London welcomed her. Her reputation spread both in Europe and at home.

In 1776, her poem "To His Excellency George Washington," honoring Washington's appointment as commander in chief of the Continental Army, earned her more praise and the thanks of Washington himself. Throughout her verses, Wheatley celebrated the ideals for which the young republic stood.

> Auspicious Heaven shall fill with fav'ring Gales,
> Where e'er *Columbia* spreads her swelling sails:
> To every Realm shall *Peace* her Charms display,
> And Heavenly *Freedom* spread her golden Ray.

Wheatley was mindful that millions of African Americans remained enslaved. "In every human breast, God has implanted a principle, which we call love of freedom," she wrote. "It is impatient of oppression, and pants for deliverance." Decades later, abolitionists revived her poems as a reminder of that universal love of liberty. Phillis Wheatley thus left a legacy that struck a blow for freedom.

ISRAEL PUTNAM

$\mathcal{C}$ onnecticut patriot Israel Putnam was a successful farmer and tavern keeper at the outset of the Revolutionary War. He had already seen more than his share of fighting. During the French and Indian War, he had been captured and would have been burned alive if a French officer had not intervened. He took part in campaigns against Fort Ticonderoga and Montreal, and in 1762 survived a shipwreck off Cuba during a mission.

On April 20, 1775, Putnam and his son Daniel were plowing in a field in Brooklyn, Connecticut, when a messenger galloped into the village with news that the British had fired on the American militia at Lexington, Massachusetts. At once Putnam mounted a horse to spread the alarm in neighboring towns and consult with local leaders. Then came news of fighting at Concord, and a call for "every man who is fit and willing" to come to their countrymen's aid.

Without stopping to rest or even change the checkered farmer's frock he'd been wearing when he left his plow, Putnam rode through the night to Cambridge, Massachusetts, near Boston, to join colonial soldiers there. By the time he reached his destination, he'd ridden one hundred miles in eighteen hours.

Two months later, Putnam commanded troops at Bunker's Hill (Breed's Hill), where he reportedly told his men, "Don't fire until you see the whites of their eyes!" Like the ancient Roman Cincinnatus, who also left his plow standing in a field when called to duty, Putnam never hesitated when his country needed him.

A monument to Israel Putnam at Brooklyn, Connecticut, reads: "Patriot, remember the heritages received from your forefathers and predecessors. Protect and perpetuate them for future generations of your countrymen."

MOUNT VERNON

*O*n May 7 in 1775, George Washington was traveling north, having left his home at Mount Vernon, Virginia, to attend the Second Continental Congress in Philadelphia. As he rode along, his thoughts were pulled in opposite directions. Ahead, war loomed—fighting had broken out at Lexington and Concord. Behind him, at his beloved plantation, the fields were full of green wheat and newly planted corn. Herring were running in the river, and the gardens were in bloom. He was not sure when he would be able to return.

Washington inherited Mount Vernon in 1761 from his half brother Lawrence, who had named the estate in honor of Admiral Edward Vernon, Lawrence's commander in the British Navy. The plantation eventually covered about eight thousand acres, and the columned house, atop a bluff overlooking the Potomac River, was one of Virginia's finest. Washington was keenly interested in farming and never tired of trying different crops and breeding livestock.

He could not have known, as he rode north, that he would have to spend years away from his plantation, first as commander of the army, later as president. "It is my full intention to devote my life and fortune in the cause we are engaged in, if need be," he wrote his brother John in 1775. But he always yearned for Mount Vernon.

When the long years of service were finally over, he happily retired to his home. "At the age of sixty-five I am recommencing my agricultural pursuits and rural amusements, which at all times have been the most pleasing occupation of my life, and most congenial with my temper," he wrote in 1797.

Washington was able to live his last years at Mount Vernon, where he died in 1799. He and his wife, Martha, are buried in a simple hillside tomb there.

THE US ARMY ORIGINS AND FLAG

*J*une 1775 brought the birth of the US Army. On June 10, 1775, in the aftermath of Lexington and Concord, John Adams urged the Continental Congress to form a Continental Army to take charge of colonial militia facing the British at Boston. On June 14, 1775 (considered the US Army's official birthday), Congress passed a resolution "that six companies of expert riflemen be immediately raised in Pennsylvania, two in Maryland, and two in Virginia," and that they "shall march and join the army near Boston." The next day, June 15, Congress made George Washington commander in chief of the new force. The Army is the oldest of the six major branches of the US Armed Forces (Army, Navy, Air Force, Marines, Coast Guard, and Space Force).

The US Army flag, adopted in 1956, is a white flag bearing a blue design that dates to the Revolutionary War. A Roman breastplate (symbol of strength and defense) stands at the center. A sword rises out of the neck opening, and on its point rests a Phrygian cap (symbol of liberty). A drum, musket, bayonet, cannon, cannonballs, flags, and other army implements surround the breastplate. Above, a rattlesnake holds a scroll with the motto This We'll Defend. Below, a red scroll reads "United States Army." And at the bottom, the date 1775 signifies the year the Army was created.

ABIGAIL ADAMS

Shortly after the Battle of Bunker Hill, Abigail Adams wrote one of the many letters she penned to her husband, John, then in Philadelphia serving in the Second Continental Congress. On a hill near her farm with her young son, Johnny, she had watched the smoke of the battle rising above Charlestown. She wrote partly to tell her husband that their friend Dr. Joseph Warren had been killed in the fight.

Dearest Friend,

The Day, perhaps the decisive Day is come on which the fate of America depends. My bursting heart must find vent at my pen. I have just heard that our dear friend Dr. Warren is no more but fell gloriously fighting for his country—saying better to die honorably in the field than ignominiously hang upon the gallows. Great is our loss. He has distinguished himself in every engagement, by his courage and fortitude, by animating the soldiers and leading them on by his own example. . . .

The race is not to the swift, nor the battle to the strong, but the God of Israel is he that giveth strength and power unto his people. Trust in him at all times, ye people pour out your hearts before him. God is a refuge for us—Charleston is laid in ashes. . . . How [many ha]ve fallen we know not—the constant roar of the cannon is so [distre]ssing that we can not eat, drink, or sleep. May we be supported and sustained in the dreadful conflict. I shall tarry here till tis thought unsafe by my friends, and then I have secured myself a retreat at your brother's, who has kindly offered me part of his house. I cannot compose myself to write any further at present. I will add more as I hear further.

THE NAVY BIRTHDAY AND FLAG

*T*he US Navy celebrates its birthday on October 13, the day in 1775 that the Continental Congress authorized the outfitting of two armed vessels to cruise in search of British munitions ships.

On that day, Congress also established a Naval Committee to oversee the new navy. John Adams was a member of the committee, and although the Massachusetts representative knew little of naval affairs, he got busy making himself expert. As historian David McCullough writes, the committee "met in a rented room at Tun Tavern [in Philadelphia], and it was Adams who drafted the first set of rules and regulations for the new navy, a point of pride with him for as long as he lived."

Throughout the Revolution, Adams urged support for the tiny American fleet, telling Congress that "a navy is our natural and only defense." Over the course of the war, the Continental Navy included about fifty ships of various sizes. After the Revolution, Congress disbanded the navy, then restarted it in 1794 when it ordered the construction of six frigates.

The US Navy flag, adopted in 1959, is a dark blue flag that carries the image of a three-masted square-rigged ship underway before a fair breeze. A bald eagle and an anchor are shown in front of the ship. Navy ships do not fly the Navy flag from their masts. The banner is reserved for display purposes and is carried by honor guards during ceremonies.

THE MARINE CORPS
BIRTHDAY AND FLAG

The US Marine Corps traces its origins to November 10, 1775, during the Revolutionary War, when the Continental Congress called for two battalions of Continental Marines to be raised. Their mission was to provide security onboard Navy ships, conduct ship-to-ship fighting, and serve as landing troops. Tradition has it that the Tun Tavern in Philadelphia served as the first Marines recruiting post. The Marines' first landing, led by Captain Samuel Nicholas, came in March 1776 at New Providence, in the Bahamas, where they seized British cannons, shells, and powder.

The Marines were disbanded after the Revolutionary War, then reformed in 1798. The US Marine Corps has served in every major armed conflict in American history. As a "force in readiness," its missions range from amphibious assaults to counterterrorism operations.

The Marine Corps flag is a scarlet banner that carries a yellow and gray image of a globe (symbolizing service in any part of the world) and an anchor (a reminder of the amphibious nature of Marines' duties, and that the Marine Corps is a partner of the US Navy). An eagle stands on the globe, holding in its beak a scroll inscribed with the Marine Corps motto, Semper Fidelis ("Always Faithful"). Below, a larger scroll reads, "United States Marine Corps." The flag's design dates to 1939.

THOMAS PAINE PUBLISHES
COMMON SENSE

O n January 9, 1776, Thomas Paine published *Common Sense*, a pamphlet that set the American colonies afire with a longing for independence.

Paine was born in England to a poor family and received little schooling. For several years he drifted from job to job—corset maker, seaman, schoolteacher, customs collector, tobacco seller—without success. His prospects were few when he met Benjamin Franklin, then living in London, who suggested he go to America. Sailing across the Atlantic, Paine caught a fever and was carried ashore half dead in Philadelphia. Once recovered, letters of recommendation from Franklin helped him get a job as a magazine writer.

It has been said that Paine "had more brains than books, more sense than education, more courage than politeness, more strength than polish." But he could work magic with pen and paper. In *Common Sense* he made bold arguments that Americans should demand their freedom. "The birthday of a new world is at hand," he insisted. He attacked the idea that people must live under a king, and urged a break from Britain.

"O ye that love mankind! Ye that dare oppose, not only the tyranny, but the tyrant, stand forth!" he wrote. "Every spot of the old world is overrun with oppression. Freedom hath been hunted round the globe. Asia, and Africa, have long expelled her. Europe regards her like a stranger, and England hath given her warning to depart. O! [America] receive the fugitive, and prepare in time an asylum for mankind."

Paine's words sounded like a trumpet blast through the colonies. Thousands snatched up the pamphlet and decided that he was right. As Thomas Edison, one of America's great geniuses, wrote 150 years later, "We never had a sounder intelligence in this Republic. . . . In *Common Sense* Paine flared forth with a document so powerful that the Revolution became inevitable."

HENRY KNOX'S LONG HAUL

On March 3 in 1776, George Washington's Patriot army was in the final stages of pulling off one of the biggest surprises of the Revolutionary War, thanks to a bookseller named Henry Knox.

The opening phase of the war found the British in control of Boston. The Patriots had not been able to break the redcoats' hold on the port, and George Washington was running out of time since the enlistment terms of many of his men would soon expire.

Henry Knox, who had owned the London Book Store in Boston and read all he could on military subjects, especially artillery, made an unlikely suggestion. Three hundred miles away, at Fort Ticonderoga in New York, lay the answer to the Patriots' problem: cannons. If the Patriots could somehow get the heavy artillery to Boston—an idea that made several officers shake their heads—they could drive the British out. With Washington's blessing, Knox hurried to Ticonderoga; chose fifty-nine big guns; loaded them onto sleds pulled by horses, oxen, and men; and headed south.

Day after day, they skidded along snow-covered trails. They lurched through mud and mountainous drifts, heaved up rough hills and down steep valleys. Crossing the frozen Hudson River, the ice cracked and a huge gun broke through. Somehow the men pulled it out. In late February the "noble train of artillery" reached Boston.

During the first few days of March, Washington's army made a big racket to distract the enemy while they moved the guns into place. Early one morning, a sleepy British sentry blinked in disbelief through the dawn mists toward Dorchester Heights, where Knox's cannons, as if appearing out of nowhere, aimed straight at him. The British, realizing they could no longer hold the city, soon boarded their fleet and sailed away. Henry Knox's long haul had saved Boston. It was the first major victory of the Revolutionary War.

BETSY ROSS

*T*radition says that the first Stars and Stripes flag was the work of Betsy Ross, an upholsterer living in Philadelphia during the Revolutionary War. About June 1776, the twenty-four-year-old widow was working in her shop on Arch Street when three gentlemen called. One was George Washington, commander in chief of the Continental Army. The other two were George Ross, a signer of the Declaration of Independence and uncle of Betsy's deceased husband, and Robert Morris, also a signer of the Declaration.

Washington produced a rough sketch of a flag with thirteen red and white stripes and thirteen six-pointed stars, and asked Betsy if she could make a banner with that design. "I do not know, but I will try," she reportedly answered, and then suggested changing the stars to five points rather than six. She picked up a piece of cloth, folded it a few times, made one snip with her scissors, and out came a perfect five-point star. The men agreed to the change, and patriot Betsy Ross began the work of stitching together the first Stars and Stripes.

Betsy Ross's grandson William Canby first made this story public in 1870. Betsy was clearly an upholsterer living in Philadelphia during the Revolution, and records show that she made flags for the Pennsylvania navy. But historians question the tale of Washington's visit and her making the first American flag since they can find no evidence to back it up. Nevertheless, generations of Americans have loved the legend, and Betsy is fondly regarded as the mother of our flag.

JOHN WITHERSPOON,
PARSON AND PATRIOT

*T*here is not a single instance in history in which civil liberty was lost, and religious liberty preserved entire." So warned Presbyterian minister John Witherspoon, who on June 22, 1776, was elected to represent New Jersey in the Continental Congress in Philadelphia.

Witherspoon had emigrated from Scotland to take the post as president of the College of New Jersey (now Princeton University). Arriving in 1768 with his family and three hundred books for the college library, he threw himself into the task of building up the young school. "He laid the foundation of a course of history in the college, and the principles of taste and the rules of good writing were both happily explained by him, and exemplified in his manner," a colleague said.

As the Revolution approached, Witherspoon's Presbyterian belief that people should choose their own government put him firmly on the Patriot side. He realized the colonies would have to fight Britain. "If your cause is just, if your principles are pure, and if your conduct is prudent, you need not fear the multitude of opposing hosts," he preached.

In the Continental Congress, some delegates worried the country was not yet ripe for independence. "The country is not only ripe for the measure, but in danger of rotting for the want of it!" Witherspoon retorted. He became the only minister to sign the Declaration of Independence.

He lost a son in the Revolution, which also left the college in dire straits. After the war he tackled the job of rebuilding the school. "Do not live useless and die contemptible," he exhorted his students, who included 9 future cabinet officers, 21 senators, 39 congressmen, 3 Supreme Court justices, 12 governors, a vice president, and a president—James Madison, who was also one of five Witherspoon students at the Constitutional Convention.

CAESAR RODNEY'S RIDE

In 1999 the US mint launched a series of quarters honoring the fifty states. The back of the Delaware quarter features a man in a tricorn hat on a galloping horse. The rider is Caesar Rodney, one of Delaware's three signers of the Declaration of Independence.

Rodney was a well-to-do planter who had served in Delaware's legislature, led protests against the Stamp Tax, and organized Patriot militia before being elected to the Continental Congress. Despite such activity, he was a man of poor health. He suffered from asthma as well as skin cancer that had left his face so disfigured, he often hid one side of it behind a green silk scarf. Yet as John Adams noted, there was "fire, spirit, wit, and humor in his countenance."

Rodney was in Delaware on the evening of July 1, 1776, when he received an urgent message from Philadelphia. Congress was ready to vote on the issue of independence. Of the two other Delaware delegates, one favored and one opposed a break with England, so Rodney's vote would decide which way the colony would go—if he could get there in time.

He rode through the night, in thunder and rain, to cover the eighty miles to Philadelphia. The next day, just as Congress prepared to vote, the delegates heard hoofbeats on cobblestones, and a mud-spattered Rodney strode into the hall, still wearing his spurs, exhausted but ready to break the tie in his state's delegation by voting for independence.

On July 2, 1776, the Continental Congress made the momentous decision to break from England: "Resolved, That these United Colonies are, and of right ought to be, free and independent States." Two days later, it adopted the Declaration of Independence.

JOHN HANCOCK

*J*ohn Hancock, born January 12, 1737, was a Boston merchant and one of the richest men in America at the time of the Revolution. A fiery Patriot, he never hesitated to risk his wealth for the cause of independence. The British considered him a dangerous traitor and reportedly put a price of five hundred pounds on his head. Hancock served as president of the Continental Congress and was the first to sign the Declaration of Independence in 1776. He signed in bold letters and, according to legend, remarked as he wrote, "There! His Majesty can now read my name without glasses. And he can double the reward on my head!"

John Hancock marveled that the Lord gave this country "a name and a standing among the nations of the world." He wrote: "I hope and pray that the gratitude of [Americans'] hearts may be expressed by a proper use of those inestimable blessings, by the greatest exertions of patriotism, by forming and supporting institutions for cultivating the human understanding, and for the greatest progress of the arts and sciences, by establishing laws for the support of piety, religion and morality. . . . and by exhibiting in the great theatre of the world, those social, public and private virtues which give more dignity to a people, possessing their own sovereignty, than crowns and diadems afford to sovereign princes."

THEY RISKED ALL

On July 4, 1776, delegates to the Continental Congress in Philadelphia voted to adopt the Declaration of Independence. The men who issued that famous document realized they were signing their own death warrants, since the British would consider them traitors. Many suffered hardship during the Revolutionary War.

William Floyd of New York saw the British use his home for a barracks. His family fled to Connecticut, where they lived as refugees. After the war Floyd found his fields stripped and house damaged.

Richard Stockton of New Jersey was dragged from his bed, thrown into prison, and treated like a common criminal. His home was looted and his fortune badly impaired. He was released in 1777, but his health was broken. He died a few years later.

At age sixty-three, John Hart, another New Jersey signer, hid in the woods during December 1776 while Hessian soldiers hunted him across the countryside. He died before the war's end. The *New Jersey Gazette* reported that he "continued to the day he was seized with his last illness to discharge the duties of a faithful and upright patriot in the service of his country."

Thomas Nelson, a Virginian, commanded militia and served as governor during the Revolution. He reportedly instructed artillerymen to fire at his own house in Yorktown when he heard the British were using it as a headquarters. Nelson used his personal credit to raise money for the Patriot cause. His sacrifices left him in financial distress, and he was unable to repair his Yorktown home after the war.

Thomas Heyward, Arthur Middleton, and Edward Rutledge, three South Carolina signers, served in their state's militia and were captured when the British seized Charleston. They spent a year in a St. Augustine prison and, when released, found their estates plundered.

Such were the prices paid so we may celebrate freedom every Fourth of July.

BUT ONE LIFE TO LOSE

*N*athan Hale was teaching school in New London, Connecticut, when the American Revolution began. In July 1775 he closed his schoolhouse doors and joined the Patriot army. He was a captain by late 1776, when the British captured New York City. George Washington desperately needed to know the strength and position of the king's forces, so he asked for a volunteer to go behind enemy lines to gather information. Nathan Hale stepped forward.

Changing his uniform for a plain suit of brown clothes and taking his Yale diploma in hand, Hale disguised himself as a schoolteacher. He slipped through the British lines and gathered the needed information, which he carefully recorded in Latin and hid under the soles of his shoes.

His mission accomplished, he began to make his way back. He got past all the British guards except the last ones. They stopped him, searched, and found the secret papers. Nathan Hale was arrested and carried before the British commander, General William Howe.

Howe took one look at the young American in civilian clothes, realized he was a spy, and ordered that he be hanged the next morning. The next several hours were cruel, lonely ones for Nathan Hale. He asked for a minister. His jailor refused. He asked for a Bible. That, too, was denied.

On the morning of September 22, 1776, Hale was led to a spot not far from what is now Central Park in New York City. The British officers who saw him marveled at his calmness and dignity. In the end he stood straight and unflinching. No American can ever forget the words he uttered before they slipped the noose around his neck: "I only regret that I have but one life to lose for my country."

THE TIMES THAT TRY MEN'S SOULS

*T*homas Paine wrote these famous words in his pamphlet *The American Crisis*, dated December 23, 1776, a time when Patriot forces stood on the verge of losing the Revolutionary War. Paine implored Americans to not give up the fight. George Washington ordered that the pamphlet be read aloud to his troops on Christmas Eve 1776 before they crossed the Delaware River to launch a surprise attack at Trenton.

These are the times that try men's souls. The summer soldier and the sunshine patriot will, in this crisis, shrink from the service of his country; but he that stands it now deserves the love and thanks of man and woman. Tyranny, like hell, is not easily conquered. Yet we have this consolation with us, that the harder the conflict, the more glorious the triumph. What we obtain too cheap, we esteem too lightly: 'tis dearness only that gives every thing its value. Heaven knows how to put a proper price upon its goods, and it would be strange indeed if so celestial an article as freedom should not be highly rated. . . .

Let it be told to the future world, that in the depth of winter, when nothing but hope and virtue could survive, the city and the country, alarmed at one common danger, came forth to meet it and to repulse it. . . . I love the man that can smile in trouble, that can gather strength from distress, and grow brave by reflection. 'Tis the business of little minds to shrink; but he whose heart is firm, and whose conscience approves his conduct, will pursue his principles unto death.

HAYM SALOMON: A FINANCIAL
HERO OF THE REVOLUTION

O n January 2 in 1777, George Washington's army was busy fighting the British in the Second Battle of Trenton, New Jersey. While
Washington fought, another great patriot was hard at work behind the
scenes, aiding the American cause. You may never have heard of Haym
Salomon, but he was one of the heroes of the American Revolution. In
fact, if not for Patriots like Salomon, there would never have been a United
States.

Born in Poland, Salomon immigrated to New York City in 1772
and soon became a successful merchant and banker. He joined the Sons
of Liberty, a Patriot group, and when war broke out, he helped supply
American troops. The British arrested him in 1776 and flung him into
prison. After a while they released him, and he went straight back to
aiding the Patriots.

The British arrested Salomon again in 1778. This time they decided to
be rid of him. They sentenced him to be hanged as a rebel, but he escaped
and fled to Philadelphia.

Once again Salomon went into business as a banker, and he continued to devote his talents and wealth to the Patriot cause. American
leaders frequently turned to him for help in raising funds to support the
war. Salomon risked his assets by loaning the government money for little
or no commission. He helped pay the salaries of army officers, tapped his

own funds to supply ragged troops, and worked tirelessly to secure French aid for the Revolution.

After the war the young nation struggled to get on its feet. When the republic needed money, Salomon helped save the United States from financial collapse.

The years following the Revolution took a toll on Haym Salomon's business. At the end of his life, his wealth was gone. In fact, he died impoverished. He had poured much of his fortune into the service of his country.

LAFAYETTE AND THE SENTRY

One of this country's greatest Patriots was a French nobleman. Born to immense wealth, the Marquis de Lafayette disliked court life and longed to fight for liberty. When he was nineteen, he bought a ship and set sail from France to join the American Revolution, arriving in South Carolina on June 13, 1777.

Declaring that "the welfare of America is intimately connected with the happiness of all mankind," Lafayette volunteered to serve in the Patriot army without pay. He fought beside the American troops and suffered with them at Valley Forge. George Washington became like a father to Lafayette, and Lafayette named his son for Washington.

After the Revolution, Lafayette sailed back to France. Twice he returned to America to see his old comrades. The second trip came in 1824, when he was an old, bent man. He traveled from town to town, and everywhere crowds welcomed him as a hero.

At one reception, an old soldier in a faded uniform approached the Frenchman. Over his shoulder he carried a tattered blanket. He gave a salute and asked if Lafayette remembered Valley Forge.

"I shall never forget them," answered Lafayette.

"One bitter night," continued the soldier, "you came upon a shivering sentry. His clothes were thin, and he was near frozen. You took his musket and said, 'Go to my hut and get my blanket. Bring it to me while I keep guard.'

"The soldier obeyed your directions. When he returned to his post, you took out your sword and cut your blanket in two. One half you kept. The other you gave to the sentry. Here, General Lafayette, is half of the blanket, for I am the soldier whose life you saved."

MOLLY PITCHER

On June 29, 1778, the day after the Battle of Monmouth in New Jersey, Mary Ludwig Hays of Pennsylvania—known to her friends as Molly—stood before General Washington and received a warrant as a noncommissioned officer in return for bravery in the battle.

Like many colonial wives, Molly had joined her husband, John, when he marched off to fight during the Revolutionary War. She spent in the camps, cooking, washing, and taking care of supplies.

June 28, 1778, found John Hays manning a cannon at Monmouth on an afternoon when the temperature soared close to one hundred degrees. Gasping soldiers began to drop from thirst and exhaustion, so Molly grabbed an artillery bucket and carried water from a cool spring to the troops. According to legend, the grateful men cheered "Molly with her pitcher," and afterward she was known as Molly Pitcher.

Molly also nursed the wounded that day. At one point she hoisted an injured soldier to her shoulders and lugged him clear of a British charge. When her husband fell wounded beside his cannon, she seized the rammer staff and worked the rest of the day swabbing and loading the gun under heavy fire. An eyewitness to the battle described how "a cannon shot from the enemy passed directly between her legs without doing any other damage than carrying away all the lower part of her petticoat."

The next day, it is said, George Washington thanked the barefooted, powder-stained Molly. In 1822 the Pennsylvania legislature voted to pay her forty dollars a year in recognition of her service. Since then, the name Molly Pitcher has come to stand for all the brave women who came to their country's aid during the war for independence.

NOT YET BEGUN

September 23, 1779, brought one of the most storied battles in the history of the US Navy. It happened during the Revolutionary War. Captain John Paul Jones, in command of an aging vessel named the *Bonhomme Richard*, was cruising off England's coast when he encountered the *Serapis*, a British ship of war.

Jones engaged the enemy as night was falling. With the opening broadsides, however, two of the *Richard*'s old cannons exploded, killing crew members and ripping away a chunk of the ship's side. The *Serapis* fired broadside after broadside into the stricken *Richard*. With his ship hit below the water line and leaking badly, Jones knew his only chance was to run into the British vessel and board her decks. He managed to lock the two ships together, but the *Serapis* kept blasting away into the *Richard*'s side, setting its old timbers on fire.

The British commander asked if the *Richard* was ready to surrender. Jones flung out his famous reply: "I have not yet begun to fight!"

The British shook their heads in disbelief. The Americans fought on. One of them managed to toss a grenade down an open hatch on the *Serapis*'s deck. The grenade hit some gunpowder, and explosions ripped through the British ship. Both vessels were now drifting wrecks. Still Jones refused to give in. After more than three and a half hours of savage battle by moonlight, the British commander surrendered. The victorious Americans boarded the *Serapis* and watched as the *Richard* disappeared beneath the waves.

Today, when the going gets tough, Americans remember the words of Captain John Paul Jones: "I have not yet begun to fight!"

JANE THOMAS'S RIDE

In the summer of 1775 Patriots in the foothills of western South Carolina organized to fight for independence. The frontiersmen called themselves the Spartan Regiment after the ancient Greek city-state famous for its warriors, and they chose as their leader Col. John Thomas, a sturdy Welsh pioneer. Even after the British captured Charleston, over-ran much of the state, and threw Colonel Thomas in prison, the Spartan Regiment refused to give in.

In July 1780, John Thomas's wife, Jane, was visiting her husband at the settlement of Ninety- Six, where he was confined, when a conversation between several Loyalist women caught her ear. One of them mentioned that Loyalist forces were planning a surprise raid for the next night against a Patriot camp at Cedar Springs. The information startled Jane. It was the place where her son, John Thomas Jr. was organizing his men.

Realizing there was no time to lose, she started out early the next morning, July 12. It was sixty miles to Cedar Springs, but Jane Thomas, nearly sixty years old, pushed her horse through the enemy-infested back-country. By evening she had reached her son's camp.

John Thomas Jr. wasted no time. The Patriots built up their campfires and slipped into the woods. The Loyalists soon arrived and rushed into the camp, expecting to find the hapless rebels asleep in their blankets. Instead, they met a sharp volley of musket balls. In the light of the camp-fires, they made easy targets for the Patriot backwoodsmen. The Loyalists retreated, leaving behind several dead. Thanks to Jane Thomas, the Battle of Cedar Springs helped launch a resurgence of Patriot fortunes in South Carolina, and brought a much-needed boost in morale.

BENEDICT ARNOLD
COMMITS TREASON

On September 21, 1780, General Benedict Arnold betrayed his country when he gave the British information that could allow them to capture the American fort at West Point on the Hudson River in New York.

At the time, Americans regarded Arnold as a hero for his bravery in the Revolutionary War. He had fought with daring skill at Fort Ticonderoga, Quebec, Valcour Island, and Saratoga. But he grew resentful at promotions other officers received, and he hungered for money to support the lifestyle he enjoyed with his young wife, the beautiful young Peggy Shippen. Arnold began exchanging secret messages with the enemy, offering betrayal in exchange for money and high rank in the British army.

On the night of September 21, he sealed the traitorous deal when he met with Major John André, aide to the commander of all British forces in North America, and handed him detailed information on West Point, which Arnold commanded. Arnold returned to the fort while André, disguised in civilian's clothes, made his way toward the British lines.

Two days later, Patriot militiamen stopped André and were shocked to discover who he was—and that he carried details about West Point in his boots, including some papers in Arnold's handwriting. Arnold was at breakfast when he received word of André's capture. He quickly excused himself, boarded his barge, and escaped to a British warship anchored in the Hudson—aptly named HMS *Vulture*.

Arnold fought for the British for the rest of the Revolution, leading troops that burned Richmond, Virginia, and New London, Connecticut. After the war he went to England, where he died in 1801, scorned by many even there. Like almost all traitors, Arnold acted not for any ideals, but for personal gain, and he earned himself the most infamous name in American history.

THE SWAMP FOX

On the night of September 29, 1780, militia loyal to King George III were camped on Black Mingo Creek in coastal South Carolina when a Patriot force materialized out of the darkness. The surprised Tories put up a sharp defense but soon fled across the Santee River, leaving behind their supplies and ammunition. Francis Marion had struck again.

One of the heroes of the American Revolution, Marion was a short, quiet man who wore a sword so seldom drawn it rusted in its scabbard. His men knew the secret paths of the low- country swamps, and like phantoms they could appear out of cypress mazes for quick surprise attacks against much larger forces before melting away to the dark recesses of their forest retreats. Most were farmers, fighting without pay. Few had uniforms of any kind. They were always short on guns, ammunition, and food, but they fought with the zeal of true Patriots.

Marion's guerrilla warfare kept the British in a constant state of confusion and alarm. With grudging respect, the redcoats began to refer to him as the Swamp Fox. It is said that one day Marion invited a British officer to dinner in his camp under a flag of truce and served a meal of fire-baked potatoes on a slab of bark, with vinegar and water to wash it down. His guest was surprised at how little the Patriots had to eat. "But surely, General," he inquired, "this can't be your usual fare?"

"Indeed, sir, it is," Marion replied, "and we are fortunate on this occasion, entertaining company, to have more than our usual allowance."

The story goes that the British officer was so overcome by the Americans' determination and sacrifice that he resigned his commission and sailed back to England.

A DEVIL OF A WHIPPING

On January 17, 1781, Patriots under Brig. Gen. Daniel Morgan defeated a British force at the Battle of Cowpens in South Carolina, a crucial victory in the American Revolution.

Morgan was a rough-and-tumble fellow. As a young man in Virginia, he had worked as a wagoner, driving supplies to settlers west of the Blue Ridge Mountains. During the French and Indian War, while driving wagons for the British, he offended a British officer, who struck him with the flat of his sword. Morgan decked the officer and was sentenced to five hundred lashes. In later years, he liked to say that the British miscounted and gave him only 499, and that they still owed him one.

During the Revolution, Morgan fought at Quebec and Saratoga. In 1780, he headed south to help fight the British in the Carolina backcountry.

Tarleton, a brilliant commander, was determined to destroy Morgan's army. He once declared that "these miserable Americans must be taught their places!" The Americans viewed Tarleton as a butcher because his troops had been known to slaughter men who tried to surrender.

When Morgan realized that Tarleton was on his trail, he sent word to local militia: meet at the Cowpens, a frontier pasturing ground. The night before the battle, "the Old Wagoner" moved among his troops, bucking them up and showing them the whipping scars on his back. By dawn he had perhaps 1,500 men carefully placed on the field.

Tarleton's fearsome dragoons charged straight into a trap. The Americans managed to surround the attackers, killing or capturing most of Tarleton's men. Tarleton escaped. But the battle was a staggering blow to the British—"A devil of a whipping," as Morgan put it—and helped turn the tide of the war.

THE PRESIDENT WITH
SHOOT IN HIS EYES

*A*ndrew Jackson, the first US president born in a log cabin, was the son of poor Scots-Irish immigrants who scratched a living from the soil of the South Carolina backcountry. His father died about two weeks before he was born, leaving the strong-willed mother, Elizabeth, to raise the Jackson boys. During the Revolutionary War, thirteen-year-old Andy joined the Patriot militia as an orderly and courier.

On April 10, 1781, the militia had gathered at a Presbyterian church when British troops surprised them. Andy and his brother Robert escaped into the woods, only to be captured the next morning at a nearby cabin. A Tory officer ordered Andy to clean his boots, and the fiery boy shot back: "Sir, I am a prisoner of war and claim to be treated as such!" The furious officer brought his sword down on the young Patriot's head, leaving a scar he carried the rest of his life.

He grew up with the frontier—saddlemaker, schoolteacher, lawyer, planter, land speculator, Indian fighter, US congressman, senator, judge, general, hero of the Battle of New Orleans. "He knew little grammar and many scars, few classics and many fast horses," the writer Carl Sandburg observed.

While a judge in Tennessee, he sent a succession of deputies to apprehend a huge man wanted for a heinous crime. They all returned empty-handed, so Jackson himself arrested the criminal. Asked why he finally surrendered, the man said, "I looked him in the eye, and I saw shoot. And there wasn't shoot in nary other eye in the crowd."

When Old Hickory was elected the seventh US president, frontiersmen rode hundreds of miles to join the inaugural party, overrunning the White House with muddy boots. Refined ladies and gents said it was the beginning of mob rule. Jackson knew better. He knew it was just American democracy on its way to growing up.

THE PATRIOT WHO
BURNED HER HOME

*D*uring the Revolutionary War, British forces seized the spacious home of Rebecca Motte on the Congaree River in South Carolina. Motte, a wealthy widow, was forced to take up residence in a smaller nearby house while about 175 British soldiers fortified her home, surrounding it with a trench and parapet.

From May 8 to May 12, 1781, a Patriot force led by Francis Marion and Lighthorse Harry Lee laid siege to Fort Motte, as the British called their compound. Marion and Lee called on Lt. Daniel McPherson, the British commander, to surrender, but he refused. The Patriots soon concluded that to get the British out, they would have to set fire to the house. When Lee broke the news to Mrs. Motte, she responded that she was "gratified with the opportunity of contributing to the good of her country, and should view the approaching scene with delight."

The widow produced a bow and set of arrows and told Lee to put them to use. The Patriots shot flaming arrows at the roof, setting it on fire and forcing a surrender. Then they quickly climbed to the top of the house and managed to put out the flames. That evening, in the tradition of true Southern hospitality, Rebecca Motte served dinner to both the American and British officers in her dining room.

JACK JOUETT'S RIDE

They call him the Paul Revere of the South. His ride isn't so well remembered, but it was every bit as daring.

By June 1781, late in the Revolutionary War, the British army had overrun much of Virginia. Patriot-turned-traitor Benedict Arnold had pillaged his way up the James River to Richmond, forcing Governor Thomas Jefferson and the legislature to flee west to Charlottesville. Lord Cornwallis ordered Col. Banastre Tarleton to lead a surprise raid on Charlottesville to capture Jefferson, Patrick Henry, Richard Henry Lee, and other assemblymen. "Bloody Ban" set out with about 250 mounted troops to nab the unsuspecting Virginians.

On the night of June 3, Captain Jack Jouett of the Virginia militia was at the Cuckoo Tavern in Louisa County (asleep on the lawn, according to some accounts) when the passing cavalry awakened him. Guessing what they were up to, twenty-seven-year-old Jouett leaped on his horse and galloped off toward Charlottesville, about forty miles away. The British were on the main road, so the six-foot-four Jouett had to take trails through the hilly backwoods, a near-full moon his only light to guide him through the underbrush.

He arrived at Monticello, Jefferson's home, in the early hours of June 4. After rousing the occupants and accepting a glass of Madeira from the grateful governor, he dashed on to nearby Charlottesville. Jefferson took his time leaving Monticello. He "breakfasted at leisure" with his guests, he later recalled, then collected important papers. When he looked through a telescope and saw British troops swarming the streets of Charlottesville, he jumped on a horse and plunged into the woods.

Jack Jouett, meanwhile, had spread the alarm in town, enabling most of the legislators to get away. Tarleton's raid was foiled, and the Patriots dodged what would have been a serious blow.

JAMES FORTEN,
FREEDOM FIGHTER

ames Forten, born in 1766 in Philadelphia, was the grandson of a slave but the son of free blacks. As a boy, he heard the Declaration of Independence read to the people of Philadelphia, and when he was fourteen, he went to sea to fight the British aboard a privateer named the *Royal Louis* under the command of Stephen Decatur.

In October 1781 the *Royal Louis* was captured by the British warship *Amphion*. Forten faced grave danger: the British often sold black prisoners of war to slave traders. But he befriended the British captain's son in a game of marbles, and the captain took such a liking to the young American that he offered to take him to England.

Forten would have none of that. "I have been taken prisoner for the liberties of my country, and never will prove a traitor to her interest!" he replied. So he spent the next seven months on a disease-ridden prison ship before being released in a prisoner exchange.

After the Revolution, Forten went to work for a Philadelphia sailmaker. Two years later he became foreman of the shop, and in 1798 he was able to buy the business. He invented a device that helped seamen handle sails, and his business prospered. In time he became a wealthy man.

What did Forten do with his success? He used it to protect and better his country. During the War of 1812, he recruited blacks to help defend Philadelphia. He later helped organize the American Anti-Slavery Society and contributed money to the abolitionist newspaper the *Liberator*. He aided runaway slaves on their way north, and extended a helping hand to all manner of people, black and white.

Forten did not live to see the end of slavery, but he believed it would come. He helped set his country on the road toward freedom for all Americans.

BETTY ZANE

On September 12, 1782, some 250 Indians and 40 British soldiers watched in surprise as the gate of a fort they had surrounded creaked open and a teenage girl darted out. Some of the Indians laughed and called "Squaw!" while the girl ran quickly but coolly across a field toward a cabin sixty yards away and disappeared inside.

Fort Henry, built in 1774 on the Ohio River, protected families settling what is now northern West Virginia. During the Revolutionary War, the British encouraged Indian assaults such as the 1782 attack.

By the second day of the siege, the desperate pioneers inside Fort Henry were running out of gunpowder. Sixteen-year-old Betty Zane volunteered to fetch more from the cabin of her brother, Colonel Ebenezer Zane, where other settlers were holding out.

Betty realized that, since she was a girl, the attackers wouldn't give her trouble on the run to the cabin. The return trip would be something else. When she emerged from the cabin with a tablecloth slung over her shoulder, the besiegers immediately guessed that it was full of gunpowder, and they opened fire.

Bullets "hissed close to her ears and cut the grass in front of her," wrote Western writer Zane Grey, a descendent of Colonel Zane. "They pattered like hail on the stockade-fence, but still untouched, unharmed, the slender brown figure sped toward the gate." Betty reached the fort safely, enabling the defenders to win one of the last battles of the Revolution. The city of Wheeling has taken Fort Henry's place, but the closing lines of an old poem recall the girl's courage.

Upon those half-cleared, rolling lands,
A crowded city proudly stands;
But of the many who reside
By green Ohio's rushing tide,
Not one has lineage prouder than
(Be he poor or rich) the man
Who boasts that in his spotless strain
Mingles the blood of Betty Zane.

WHAT IS AN AMERICAN?

When French-American J. Hector St. John de Crèvecoeur died on November 12, 1813, he left behind a vivid portrait of life on the eighteenth-century American frontier. Crèvecoeur had emigrated to the New World in 1755 and eventually settled on a farm in New York. His impressions, published in England in 1782 as *Letters from an American Farmer*, still offer insights about the American character:

> What then is the American, this new man? . . . He is an American who, leaving behind him all his ancient prejudices and manners, receives new ones from the new mode of life he has embraced, the new government he obeys, and the new rank he holds. He becomes an American by being received in the broad lap of our great Alma Mater. Here individuals of all nations are melted into a new race of men, whose labors and posterity will one day cause great changes in the world. Americans are the western pilgrims who are carrying along with them that great mass of arts, sciences, vigor, and industry which began long since in the East; they will finish the great circle. . . . The American ought therefore to love this country much better than that wherein either he or his forefathers were born. Here the rewards of his industry follow with equal steps the progress of his labor . . . without any part being claimed, either by a despotic prince, a rich abbot, or a mighty lord. . . . The American is a new man, who acts upon new principles; he must therefore entertain new ideas and form new opinions. From involuntary idleness, servile dependence, penury, and useless labor, he has passed to toils of a very different nature, rewarded by ample subsistence. This is an American.

THE FATHER OF THE
CONSTITUTION

On August 8 in 1787, delegates to the Constitutional Convention in Philadelphia were in the midst of the eleventh week of a long, hot summer spent hammering out a new government for the United States. One young delegate from Virginia never missed a session. He sat up front so he could hear every word and take notes on every speech. At the end of each day, he went back to his boardinghouse to read over what had been said and write out new arguments.

The young Virginian was James Madison. A graduate of the College of New Jersey (now Princeton University), he was a short, slight man with a soft voice. Someone once observed that he seemed "no bigger than half a piece of soap." But his influence on this country was profound.

Madison had come to Philadelphia with a plan for a central government with three branches. He envisioned a nation where citizens would vote for their representatives. He had spent months studying ancient democracies and republics, and he knew that the strength of the government must come not from harsh laws or armies, but from the people.

That summer, Madison made more than 150 speeches in his soft voice. His fellow delegates sometimes had to shout "Louder!" but when he spoke, they knew he would bring sound reason to the debate. Madison answered questions and proposed solutions. He worked on every detail. At the end of the convention, the new Constitution that the delegates signed largely followed his plan.

Madison spent the rest of his life making sure the Constitution worked. His labors included cowriting the Federalist Papers, authoring the Bill of Rights, and serving as congressman, secretary of state, and the fourth US president. For his ideas and hard work, history remembers him as the Father of the Constitution.

ALEXANDER HAMILTON

*A*lexander Hamilton was born an orphan from the Caribbean island of Nevis, he rose with astounding speed to become an aide-de-camp to George Washington, a hero of the Revolutionary War, and a member of the Constitutional Convention. As the first secretary of the treasury, he helped build the new nation's financial systems. As a leader of the Federalist Party, he helped create our political system. He was never president of the United States, but he shaped the new American nation as few other Founding Fathers did.

Because he argued for a strong central government, Hamilton is often seen as an anti-democratic figure. But he could write as memorably of natural law and human rights as any of the Founders. "The sacred rights of mankind are not to be rummaged for among old parchments or musty records," he wrote. "They are written, as with a sunbeam, in the whole volume of human nature, by the hand of the Divinity itself and can never be erased or obscured by mortal power."

One of Hamilton's greatest contributions was to help persuade Americans to accept the Constitution. With James Madison and John Jay, he wrote the Federalist Papers, a series of brilliant newspaper essays urging the Constitution's ratification. Many people predicted that the new plan for government would not work. But Hamilton believed his countrymen should put aside their differences and give it a try. "The system, though it may not be perfect in every part, is, upon the whole, a good one," he reminded them. "I never expect to see a perfect work from imperfect man." If not for Hamilton's brilliant arguments and efforts, the thirteen former colonies might have gone their separate ways.

MARTHA WASHINGTON

Martha Washington, America's first First Lady, was a dignified, gentle woman. Abigail Adams called her "one of those unassuming characters which create Love and Esteem."

One visitor described meeting Martha: "We dressed ourselves in our most elegant ruffles and silks, and were introduced to her ladyship. And, don't you think, we found her knitting, and with a checked apron on! She received us very graciously and easily, but after the compliments were over, she resumed her knitting."

Like her husband, Mrs. Washington loved home life at Mount Vernon. But during the Revolution, whenever the Continental Army was in winter camp, she left home to join her husband and lift the troops' spirits. "I never in my life knew a woman so busy from early morning until late at night as was Lady Washington, providing comforts for the sick soldiers," recalled one woman in Valley Forge. "Every fair day she might be seen, with basket in hand . . . going among the huts seeking the keenest and most needy sufferers, and giving all the comfort to them in her power."

Martha was a warm, hospitable First Lady, but she wasn't overly fond of the role. "I think I am more like a state prisoner than anything else," she confided to a niece. Yet her willingness to serve equaled her husband's. "I cannot blame him for having acted according to his ideas of duty in obeying the voice of his country. I am still determined to be cheerful and happy, in whatever situation I may be; for I have also learned from experience that the greater part of our happiness or misery depends upon our dispositions, and not upon our circumstances."

THE COAST GUARD
BIRTHDAY AND FLAG

*T*he Coast Guard flag is a white flag bearing the national coat of arms, which also appears on the Great Seal of the United States. Above the arms are the words "United States Coast Guard," and below is the Coast Guard's motto, *Semper Paratus*, which means "always prepared."

The flag carries the date 1790 because on August 4 of that year, Congress established the Revenue Cutter Service with a fleet of ten cutters to enforce tariff laws. From 1790 to 1798, the Revenue Cutter Service was the nation's only armed force on the sea. In the early days of the republic, its cutters chased smugglers, battled pirates, captured slave ships, and fought in the War of 1812.

In 1915 the Revenue Cutter Service merged with the US Life-Saving Service to form the US Coast Guard, whose mission included the duty for which the Coast Guard is now renowned: coming to the aid of stricken ships. Over the following decades, Coast Guard cutter activities ranged from rescuing hurricane victims to chasing rumrunners during Prohibition and patrolling for enemy subs during World War II.

The Coast Guard is part of the Department of Homeland Security during peacetime. In times of war, it becomes part of the Navy. Its many missions include search and rescue operations, enforcing maritime laws, keeping ports secure, intercepting illegal immigrants, catching drug smugglers, and defending the nation from terrorism.

BENJAMIN BANNEKER

To Benjamin Banneker, born in 1731 in Baltimore County, Maryland, the words "all men are created" had potent meaning. A free black and descendent of former slaves, Banneker had been limited to a few scattered months of education at a one-room Quaker school. But from an early age he exhibited a mathematical and scientific genius. As a young farmer, he decided to build a clock that struck the hours, even though he had never seen one before. He made it entirely from wood, carving the gears and wheels with a pocketknife, and it kept time for more than forty years.

At age fifty-seven, Banneker borrowed some books and a telescope from a neighbor, George Ellicott, and taught himself astronomical calculations that allowed him to predict a 1789 solar eclipse. In 1791 he helped lay out the boundaries of the nation's new capital, the District of Columbia.

From 1792 to 1797 he furnished the astronomical tables for *Benjamin Banneker's Pennsylvania, Delaware, Maryland and Virginia Almanack*. The yearly almanacs spread his fame as the "African astronomer," and abolitionists used them to fight antiblack stereotypes.

Banneker sent his first almanac to Secretary of State Thomas Jefferson, along with a letter reminding him of the ideals he'd expressed in the Declaration of Independence. He wrote Jefferson that he hoped "that your sentiments are concurrent with mine, which are, that one universal Father hath given being to us all; and that he hath . . . afforded us all the same sensations and endowed us all with the same faculties."

Jefferson's cordial reply expressed satisfaction "to see such proofs as you exhibit." A more cogent observation came from Maryland's James McHenry, a signer of the Constitution. Benjamin Banneker's work, he wrote, showed that "the powers of the mind are disconnected to the color of the skin."

ABIGAIL ADAMS

*M*y dearest friend," wrote Abigail Adams on January 22, 1797, "We have had this day something very like a snowstorm. It has banked some though not very deep. . . ." So ran one of hundreds of letters she penned to her husband, John, during their fifty-four-year marriage.

When John began to aid the Patriot cause, Abigail stood beside him, even though rebellion threatened his livelihood as a lawyer. When he was asked to serve in the Massachusetts Assembly, she made ready to share whatever dangers would come, though it meant the king might consider her family traitors.

While John was in Philadelphia at meetings of the Continental Congress, Abigail stayed home in Quincy, Massachusetts, to run their farm. She tended the garden and orchards, looked after the livestock, sold milk and butter, and taught their children (one of them, John Quincy, a future president). When war came to Massachusetts, Abigail traded for food since American money was worthless. She took refugees into her house and calmed her children as gunfire sounded across the hills.

While John worked in Congress, she wrote to him almost daily, encouraging him, keeping up his spirits, giving advice, and sending him war news from New England.

Twice Abigail saw John cross the sea to represent the new American government abroad. It meant years of being apart. When John grew so miserable he could not go on without her, she sailed to Europe to join him.

When John became the second president, Abigail worked by his side, giving her counsel, helping him with his papers and speeches, and entertaining dignitaries. She opened the brand-new White House, which at that time was an unfinished mansion in a swamp.

When we count this nation's blessings, it is good to remember that without women like Abigail Adams, there would never have been a United States.

FIRST IN THE HEARTS

On December 14, 1799, George Washington died at Mount Vernon at age sixty-seven, two days after being caught out in sleet and snow while riding over his farms. Congress asked Virginia statesman Henry "Light-Horse Harry" Lee to eulogize the nation's hero. Lee's words about his friend have endured for over two centuries:

> First in war, first in peace and first in the hearts of his countrymen, he was second to none in the humble and endearing scenes of private life. Pious, just, humane, temperate and sincere—uniform, dignified and commanding—his example was as edifying to all around him as were the effects of that example lasting. . . . Correct throughout, vice shuddered in his presence and virtue always felt his fostering hand. The purity of his private character gave effulgence to his public virtues. . . . Such was the man for whom our nation mourns.

Fellow Virginian Thomas Jefferson wrote of George Washington's character:

> His mind was great and powerful, without being of the very first order; his penetration strong, though not so acute as that of a Newton, Bacon, or Locke; and as far as he saw, no judgment was ever sounder. . . . He was incapable of fear, meeting personal dangers with the calmest unconcern. Perhaps the strongest feature in his character was prudence, never acting until every circumstance, every consideration, was maturely

weighed; refraining if he saw a doubt, but, when once decided, going through with his purpose, whatever obstacles opposed. His integrity was most pure, his justice the most inflexible I have ever known. . . . It may truly be said that never did nature and fortune combine more perfectly to make a great man.

JOHNNY APPLESEED

John Chapman, better known as Johnny Appleseed, was born in 1774 in Leominster, Massachusetts. So much lore surrounds his life, it is difficult to separate fact from fiction, but Chapman was a real man and a folk hero during his own lifetime.

According to one story, he got the idea to plant apple trees after a horse kicked him in the head, which gave him a vision of heaven filled with apple orchards in bloom. Be that as it may, by around 1800 he had headed west and was seen drifting down the Ohio River past Steubenville, Ohio, with two canoes lashed together and loaded with apples from cider presses in western Pennsylvania. He used the cargo to plant trees.

Chapman was a wanderer and an eccentric. He reportedly wore a coffee sack for a shirt and a tin pot for a hat. But he was also a smart businessman in his own way. His strategy was to travel the frontier and plant nurseries where he thought pioneers would settle. By the time they showed up, his young trees were ready to be sold or bartered. He walked thousands of miles, always shoeless, planting and tending orchards scattered through Ohio, Indiana, and Illinois.

It didn't take long for folks to give him the nickname Johnny Appleseed. Stories of his strange kindness are legion. It is said he once put out his campfire because the blaze burned a mosquito. Pioneer families welcomed him on his travels, and he was likely to pull out his Bible and preach news "right fresh from Heaven."

When Chapman died in 1845, he owned about 1,200 acres of nurseries, much of it prime real estate. Far more valuable are the legends he left behind of humble, barefoot Johnny Appleseed.

SACAGAWEA

*O*n May 14, 1805, the Lewis and Clark expedition was pushing up the Missouri River when a sudden squall hit the sail of one of their boats and swamped it. Captains Meriwether Lewis and William Clark, ashore at the time, looked on in horror as "our papers, instruments, books, medicine, a great part of our merchandise, and in short almost every article indispensably necessary to . . . insure the success of the enterprise" threatened to float away.

While the men struggled to get the boat to land, the expedition's only female member quickly and calmly plucked the supplies from the icy river. "The Indian woman, to whom I ascribe equal fortitude and resolution with any person on board at the time of accident, caught and preserved most of the light articles which were washed overboard," Lewis wrote in his journal. Six days later, the grateful captains named "a handsome river of about fifty yards in width" in Montana after Sacagawea, the young Shoshone woman.

Sacagawea (whose name means "bird woman"), the wife of a French trader, was hired by Lewis and Clark as an interpreter. Strapping her baby son on her back, she trekked west with the explorers on their famous "Voyage of Discovery" to the Pacific. Along the way she helped communicate with Native Americans. In the Rockies, the Corps of Discovery met a band of Shoshone whose chief turned out to be Sacagawea's brother. She helped persuade them to provide horses needed to cross the mountains.

Sacagawea's fortitude and perseverance have made her a favorite American heroine.

FULTON'S FOLLY

*I*n 1787 young Robert Fulton of Pennsylvania traveled to London to study painting. The Industrial Revolution was beginning in Britain, as well as a revolution in transportation, so the American heard much excited talk of steam engines and canals. Fulton had an inventive mind—as a boy, he had made skyrockets and designed a hand-turned paddle wheel for a rowboat. In England he decided to put aside painting and try his hand at scientific pursuits. He invented a machine for making rope, and another for dredging canal channels. Then he built a submarine called the *Nautilus*, which could dive twenty-five feet underwater, and tried to sell it to Napoleon. The conqueror said no, but Fulton met Robert Livingston, the American ambassador to France, and the two men built a steamboat that chugged up and down the Seine River in Paris.

Returning to the United States, Fulton determined to build a 130-foot steam-powered paddleboat on the Hudson River. On August 17, 1807, a crowd gathered to watch him launch the "boat driven by a tea kettle" on its maiden voyage from New York City to Albany. Most called it "Fulton's folly" and predicted it would explode. "There were not, perhaps, thirty persons in the city who believed that the boat would ever move one mile per hour," Fulton wrote.

He lit the boiler, and the vessel went puffing up the river at the astounding speed of four miles per hour while people cheered. The famous boat came to be known as the *Clermont* after the Hudson River estate of Fulton's partner, Robert Livingston.

Robert Fulton did not invent the steamboat. But his *Clermont*, the first commercially successful paddle steamer, ushered in a new age in transportation.

ELIZABETH ANN SETON

*E*lizabeth Ann Seton, the first American-born saint, was born in New York City on August 28, 1774. She grew up in a well-to-do family and married William Seton, a wealthy young New York shipping merchant. Elizabeth had five children, enjoyed a privileged social position, and devoted herself to several charitable activities.

In 1803 her world came crashing down around her. William's shipping business went bankrupt, and he developed tuberculosis. They sailed to Italy in search of a healthier climate, but William soon died. While waiting for passage back to the United States, Elizabeth stayed with an Italian family and was deeply impressed with their devout Catholic faith.

Elizabeth returned to New York with little money. She soon made a decision that made her life even harder—she decided to become a Catholic. It was a time in American history when Catholics often suffered great prejudice. Rejected by family and friends, she struggled to support her children.

A rector in Baltimore heard of her plight and invited her to establish a school for girls there. In 1808 Elizabeth embarked on a remarkable new life. Settling in Baltimore, she started the Paca Street School, the country's first Catholic elementary school. A year later she founded the Sisters of Charity of St. Joseph's, a religious community of women devoted to teaching and serving the poor. As the community grew, it opened schools and orphanages in New York and Philadelphia.

Elizabeth Seton died on January 4, 1821. Today Seton's legacy includes thousands of sisters who work in hundreds of schools, hospitals, and social service centers throughout the world. In 1975 the Roman Catholic Church declared Elizabeth Ann Seton a saint.

DON'T GIVE UP

During the War of 1812 between the United States and Britain, Captain James Lawrence sailed in command of the thirty-six-gun frigate USS *Chesapeake*. On June 1, 1813, the *Chesapeake* engaged the warship HMS *Shannon* near Boston in a ship-to-ship duel. Lawrence's crew was young and inexperienced, while the *Shannon* had one of the best-trained crews in the Royal Navy. The British guns quickly cut away the *Chesapeake*'s rigging, setting her adrift, and the king's men swarmed onto the American vessel.

Within a few minutes Captain Lawrence was mortally wounded. As he was carried below deck, he gave his last order: "Tell the men to fire faster! Don't give up the ship!"

Despite the captain's exhortation, the *Chesapeake* was soon captured. Lawrence died a few days later, leaving behind a wife and daughter.

When fellow officer Oliver Hazard Perry heard of Lawrence's death, he had his friend's dying words stitched onto a large blue banner, which he flew from his flagship, the USS *Lawrence*—named for Captain Lawrence—when he fought the British on Lake Erie in September 1813.

Perry's flag now hangs in a place of honor in Memorial Hall at the US Naval Academy in Annapolis, Maryland. The words it bears—"Don't Give Up the Ship"—have become a rallying cry of the Navy.

DOLLEY MADISON

On August 24, 1814, during the War of 1812, British troops marched on Washington, DC. Outside the city waited a ragtag American army along with President James Madison and his advisors, who had raced to the battlefield to witness the capital's defense. The crack British forces quickly overran the American lines.

Panic reigned in Washington as fleeing soldiers and statesmen began straggling through the city's streets. Many public records, including the Declaration of Independence, had already been packed into linen bags and carted off to Virginia, where they were piled in an empty house. Now the roads leading out of town began to fill with wagons carrying families and their valuables. In nearby Georgetown and Alexandria, citizens made plans to surrender at the first sight of a British officer.

First Lady Dolley Madison calmly directed last-minute details at the White House. A large portrait of George Washington hung in the dining room. It would be a disgrace if it fell into British hands. Dolley ordered two servants to bring it along, but the huge frame was screwed so tightly to the wall that no one could get it down. Minutes ticked by as they tugged and tugged, to no avail. The First Lady refused to leave without the portrait. At last someone produced a penknife and carefully cut the canvas from the frame. With the precious painting in hand, Dolley and her comrades headed toward Virginia.

Later that evening, the British entered a dark and empty Washington. The Capitol building and White House went up in flames, and the night sky glowed red as the city burned. It was the only time our nation's capital has fallen into enemy hands. The determined Americans would rebuild. In the meantime Dolley Madison had saved a piece of the national pride.

THE SANTA FE TRAIL

*E*very man will fit himself for the trip with a horse, a good rifle, and as much ammunition as the company may think necessary," William Becknell explained in a *Missouri Intelligencer* ad seeking men to accompany him west. "Every man will furnish an equal part of the fitting out for trade, and receive an equal part of the product."

Ever since Zebulon Pike wandered into Spanish territory during his explorations, Spanish officials had chased American traders out of New Mexico, which was said to be rich in silver, furs, and livestock. But in 1821, Becknell heard reports of Mexican independence from Spain, so he decided to risk a trading expedition. He set out from Franklin, Missouri, with a string of pack mules, and on November 16, 1821, after several weeks of "hardships and obstacles occurring almost daily," he arrived to a warm welcome in Santa Fe. When the traders got back to Franklin, they cut open saddlebags full of silver dollars that "clinking on the stone pavement rolled into the gutter."

Soon other exultant Missouri traders were heading west on the nine-hundred-mile Santa Fe Trail, their pack trains loaded with cottons, silks, woolens, hardware, and cutlery. They returned with pelts, hides, and Mexican silver. On the trail, they risked heat, thirst, hostile Indians, raging prairie fires, and storms that could tear wagons apart. While blazing a path across the Cimarron Desert, Becknell himself barely escaped dying of thirst by cutting open a buffalo and drinking the water in its stomach.

But the trade was good, so the traders kept coming. Pioneer families, gold-seekers, hunters, and adventurers followed along. For his role in opening the way in the Southwest, William Becknell is remembered as the Father of the Santa Fe Trail.

JAMES MONROE

James Monroe, the fifth president of the United States, was born in Westmoreland County, Virginia. Thomas Jefferson reportedly declared, "Monroe was so honest that if you turned his soul inside out there would not be a spot on it."

The son of a planter, Monroe attended the College of William and Mary in Williamsburg but abandoned his studies to fight in the Revolutionary War. He was with Washington's army on Christmas night 1776 when it crossed the Delaware River to attack the Hessians at Trenton, New Jersey. As he led a charge against enemy cannon, a musket ball ripped into his shoulder, nearly killing him. When his wounds had healed, he went back to fighting for independence.

After the war, he studied law under Thomas Jefferson and embarked on a remarkable career. He served in the Virginia Assembly, the Continental Congress, the US Senate, and twice as governor of Virginia. President Washington sent him to Paris as US minister to France. Under President Jefferson, he helped negotiate the Louisiana Purchase and served as US minister to Britain. President Madison thought so highly of Monroe that he appointed him to serve simultaneously as secretary of state and secretary of war.

Americans rewarded his tireless efforts with two terms in the White House, from 1817 to 1825. Today we most remember President Monroe for his 1823 declaration that the Western Hemisphere was off-limits to colonization by European powers. The United States would not try to seize colonial possessions, Monroe said, but it would also not permit any European nation to establish new colonies in the Americas. The Monroe Doctrine has been a pillar of American foreign policy ever since.

THE WAYS OF PROVIDENCE

A friend and political ally of Thomas Jefferson asked the retired president to give some advice to his young son, Thomas Jefferson Smith, who had been named after Jefferson. A little more than a year before he died, Jefferson composed a letter to be given to Smith when he was old enough to appreciate it. He enclosed some practical advice, such as "Pride costs us more than hunger, thirst and cold," and "When angry, count ten before you speak. If very angry, a hundred." But the most moving part of the letter consists of the following "few words":

Monticello, February 21, 1825

This letter will, to you, be as one from the dead. The writer will be in the grave before you can weigh its counsels. Your affectionate and excellent father has requested that I would address to you something which might possibly have a favorable influence on the course of life you have to run, and I too, as a namesake, feel an interest in that course. Few words will be necessary, with good dispositions on your part. Adore God. Reverence and cherish your parents. Love your neighbor as yourself, and your country more than yourself. Be just. Be true. Murmur not at the ways of Providence. So shall the life into which you have entered, be the portal to one of eternal and ineffable bliss. And if to the dead it is permitted to care for the things of this world, every action of your life will be under my regard. Farewell.

PRAISE OF LIBERTY

*N*oah Webster was born in 1758 in West Hartford, Connecticut. Generations of schoolchildren grew up studying his popular "Blue-Backed Speller," so called because of its blue cover. But his most famous work was the *American Dictionary of the English Language*, first published in 1828. At a time when even educated people spelled words however they wished, Webster's dictionary helped bring order and consistency to language. An ardent patriot, he tried to free the American language from British influences. For example, he "Americanized" the British spelling of *colour*, changing it to *color*. In his essay "On the Education of Youth in America," he argued that education in the young republic should promote love of country—an idea still good in the twenty-first century.

> But every child in America should be acquainted with his own country. He should read books that furnish him with ideas that will be useful to him in life and practice. As soon as he opens his lips, he should rehearse the history of his own country; he should lisp the praise of liberty, and of those illustrious heroes and statesmen who have wrought a revolution in her favor.

He believed that the settlement and geography of America, the history of the late revolution and of the most remarkable characters and events that distinguished it, and a compendium of the principles of the federal and provincial governments should be the principal school book in the United States. These assist people in forming attachments to the country, as well as in enlarging the understanding.

FREDERICK DOUGLASS

*F*rederick Douglass was born a slave near Easton, Maryland, in February 1818 (the exact date is uncertain). A story from his youth sums up his courage in many ways. When he was sixteen years old, his master hired him out to a farmer named Edward Covey, who had a reputation for cruelty to slaves. Covey often whipped his new field hand until Douglass was, in his own words, "broken in body, soul, and spirit."

One day Covey began to tie Douglass with a rope, intending to beat him again. "At this moment—from whence came the spirit, I don't know—I resolved to fight," Douglass later recalled. He grabbed Covey by the throat and held off his blows. The two men fell to wrestling and rolling in a barnyard until finally Covey quit. Striking a white man could bring severe punishment, but Covey told no one of the fight—he did not want people to know he could not control a sixteen-year-old slave. He never tried to whip the boy again. "My long-crushed spirit rose," Douglass remembered. "The day had passed forever when I could be a slave."

Douglass eventually escaped to the North, where he became one of the nation's most eloquent voices decrying the evils of slavery. After the Civil War he continued to write and speak for the rights of black Americans. Though often a fiery critic of his country, he was also a patriot who was determined to make it a better place. "No nation was ever called to the contemplation of a destiny more important and solemn than ours," he wrote. He spent his life working for an America that offered "justice for all men, justice now and always, justice without reservation or qualification except those suggested by mercy and love."

LINCOLN'S BUMPY ROAD

On September 9, 1836, Abraham Lincoln earned his license to practice law in Illinois—a sweet victory for a prairie lad with less than a year of formal education. Like all others, Lincoln's life was bumpy with both successes and setbacks. "I do the very best I know how, the very best I can, and I mean to keep doing so until the end," he said.

1832–Elected captain of an Illinois militia company

1832–Defeated for state legislature

1833–Failed in business

1833–Appointed postmaster of New Salem, Illinois

1834–Elected to state legislature

1835–Sweetheart died

1836–Received license to practice law in Illinois

1838–Defeated for Speaker of the Illinois House

1841–Suffered deep depression

1842–Married Mary Todd

1844–Established his own law practice

1846–Elected to US Congress

1849–Failed to get appointment to US Land Office

1850–Four-year-old son died

1855–Defeated for US Senate

1857–Earned large attorney fee in a successful case

1858–Again defeated for Senate

1860–ELECTED PRESIDENT OF THE UNITED STATES

OLD MAN ELOQUENT
AND THE *AMISTAD*

"I am too old!" protested John Quincy Adams, congressman and former president of the United States, when admirers asked him to argue a case before the US Supreme Court.

The situation was this. In 1839 the Spanish schooner *Amistad* left Havana, Cuba, for another Cuban port, carrying fifty-three African slaves. Under the leadership of an African named Cinque, the captives revolted, killed the captain, and seized the ship. They demanded to be taken back to Africa, but the *Amistad*'s navigator tricked them and sailed toward Long Island, New York. A US Navy vessel took the ship into custody and brought it to Connecticut.

Spain demanded that the US return the *Amistad* and its human cargo as the property of Spain. The administration of President Martin van Buren agreed. But Cinque and his comrades—supported by American abolitionists—insisted that they were not "property" at all, but human beings who had been kidnapped in Africa.

Now the dispute was going to the US Supreme Court, and the abolitionists wanted John Quincy Adams, known as "Old Man Eloquent," to help argue their case. Adams worried he was too rusty. He had not been in a courtroom in decades. But he finally agreed.

On February 24, 1841, a nervous Adams began presenting his argument to the justices. His voice faltered at first, but his cause brought him confidence. He pointed to a framed document on the wall. "The moment you come to the Declaration of Independence, that every man has a right to life and liberty, as an inalienable right, this case is decided. I ask nothing more on behalf of these unfortunate men than this Declaration."

The Court ruled that since the transatlantic slave trade had been banned, the Africans were free men. Old Man Eloquent won his case. For payment, he received a handsomely bound Bible from the Africans—and profound satisfaction at having struck a blow for liberty.

PRESIDENTIAL TRIVIA

*W*illiam McKinley, the twenty-fifth US president, was born in 1843 in Niles, Ohio. If you ever have the good fortune to see a five-hundred-dollar bill, you'll find him pictured on it. McKinley was the last veteran of the Civil War to serve as president. He also holds the unfortunate distinction of being one of four presidents to be assassinated. Who were the others? Read on.

Who was the first president born outside the thirteen original states?
Abraham Lincoln, in Kentucky

Who was the first president born west of the Mississippi?
Herbert Hoover, in Iowa

Who was the first president born in the twentieth century?
John F. Kennedy, 1917

Who was the tallest president?
Abraham Lincoln, 6'4"

Who was the shortest?
James Madison, 5'4"

Which presidents were father and son?
John Adams and John Quincy Adams; George H. W. Bush and George W. Bush

Which presidents were grandfather and grandson?
William Harrison and Benjamin Harrison

Which president never married?
James Buchanan

Which president was born on the Fourth of July?
Calvin Coolidge, 1872

Which presidents died on the Fourth of July?
Thomas Jefferson, 1826; John Adams, 1826; James Monroe, 1831

Which presidents were assassinated?
Abraham Lincoln, 1865; James Garfield, 1881; William McKinley, 1901; John F. Kennedy, 1963

Which survived assassination attempts?
Andrew Jackson, Theodore Roosevelt, Franklin D. Roosevelt, Harry Truman, Gerald Ford, Ronald Reagan

Other than the four assassinated, which four presidents died in office?
William Harrison, 1841; Zachary Taylor, 1850; Warren Harding, 1923; Franklin D. Roosevelt, 1945

SAMUEL MORSE STARTS A COMMUNICATIONS REVOLUTION

A s a young man, Samuel Morse set out to become a famous painter. His ambition was "to rival the genius of a Raphael, a Michelangelo, or a Titian." He studied at the Royal Academy in London and won acclaim by painting portraits of men such as President James Monroe and the Marquis de Lafayette.

In 1832, onboard a ship crossing the ocean, Morse heard another passenger describe how electricity could pass instantly over any length of wire. He began to wonder: Could messages be sent over wires with electricity? He rushed back to his cabin, took out his drawing book, and began to sketch out his idea for a telegraph.

He knew little about electricity, but he learned as he went. He used a homemade battery and parts from an old clock to build his first models. He developed a code of long and short electrical impulses—"Dots" and "dashes"—to represent letters. His invention raised the interest of Alfred Vail, a machinist who became his partner.

On January 6, 1838, the inventors were ready to test their device over two miles of wire at the Vail family ironworks in New Jersey. Vail's father scribbled *"A patient waiter is no loser"* on a piece of paper and handed it to his son. "If you can send this and Mr. Morse can read it at the other end, I shall be convinced," he said. A short time later, his words came out on the receiving end.

On May 24, 1844, an amazed crowd in the Supreme Court chambers in Washington, DC, watched Samuel Morse demonstrate his telegraph by sending a message over a wire to Baltimore, thirty-five miles away. In Morse code, he tapped out a quote from the Bible: *What hath God wrought!*

Soon telegraph lines linked countries and continents, and the world entered the age of modern communication.

THE DONNER PARTY

O n July 31, 1846, the band of settlers known as the Donner Party left Fort Bridger, Wyoming, on their journey to California, electing to take a new, untried route recommended by a promoter named Lansford Hastings. "Hastings Cutoff . . . is said to be a saving of 350 or 400 miles," wrote party member James Reed in a letter that day. It turned out to be a road to disaster.

The nucleus of the emigrant party consisted of the families of George Donner, his brother Jacob, and their friend James Reed. They had set out in April from Springfield, Illinois, with dreams of new lives in California. Others joined them, and eventually the hopeful party numbered eighty-seven people and twenty-three wagons.

Within a few days of leaving Fort Bridger, they were in trouble. Hastings Cutoff proved a tortuous route. The men had to chop a trail across the Wasatch Mountains in Utah. They ran out of water crossing the deserts. Oxen began to die, and some wagons were abandoned. The emigrants were way behind schedule when they reached the Sierra Nevada. Then came snow—eventually twenty-two feet of it—trapping them in a mountain pass in northern California.

They set up camp, hoping to ride out the winter, but provisions were dangerously low. Fifteen of them, calling themselves the "Forlorn Hope," set off across the mountains for help. Only seven survived the trek.

Four relief parties went after the stranded settlers. When the first rescuers reached their camp and called out, a few bony figures crawled out of holes in the snow. "Are you men from California, or do you come from heaven?" one emaciated woman asked. Some of the starving settlers had been forced to eat their comrades' dead bodies to survive.

Only forty-six of the eighty-seven Donner Party members lived through the cold and hunger. Their ordeal is a somber reminder of the fortitude of thousands who crossed the mountains and plains.

ELIZABETH BLACKWELL

On January 23, 1849, Elizabeth Blackwell became the first woman in the United States to receive a medical degree when she graduated from New York's Geneva Medical College.

Blackwell had emigrated with her family from England to the US at age eleven after her father's sugar refinery business failed. A few years later her father died, and she took up teaching to help support the family. The idea to become a doctor came from a dying friend. "If I could only have been treated by a lady doctor, my worst sufferings would have been spared me," she told Elizabeth. "Promise me you will at least think about it."

It was a time when most people thought women incapable of such work. More than two dozen medical schools rejected Blackwell before she was finally accepted by Geneva Medical College. She arrived on campus to discover that her admission had been something of a jest. Evidently the faculty had allowed the all-male student body to vote on her application, thinking they would never accept her. Many students thought it was a practical joke, and voted yes.

Once enrolled, Blackwell earned the admiration of her professors and classmates. She ended up graduating with top honors.

In 1851, Blackwell opened her own practice in New York City. At first most doctors shunned her, and few patients came to see her. A few years later, her sister and another female friend, who had also become doctors, joined her to open the New York Infirmary for Women and Children (now the New York Downtown Hospital). The institution served the poor and established a medical school that graduated hundreds of female doctors and nurses.

By the time Blackwell died in 1910, thousands of American women had followed in her footsteps. Today, more than half of the doctors graduating from US medical schools are women.

A WOMAN CALLED MOSES

*H*arriet Tubman was born into slavery but refused to spend her life in bondage. In 1849 she began walking north until she reached freedom. Yet her own liberty wasn't enough. During the 1850s, she ventured back into the South to guide slaves along the Underground Railroad—even though she would face severe punishment if caught.

Tubman usually traveled at night, shepherding runaway slaves through woods, fields, and swamps as they followed the North Star. She often wore disguises and sang hymns to signal others along the way.

She moved just hours ahead of fugitive slave hunters. On one rescue mission, she saw a former master walking toward her. She was carrying some live chickens, so she pulled the string around their legs until they squawked, then stooped to attend to the fluttering birds while the man passed inches away. Another time when she was on a train, she spotted a former master, so she grabbed a newspaper and pretended to read. Since the man knew that Harriet Tubman was illiterate, he did not look closely at her, and she arrived at her destination unnoticed.

During the Civil War, Tubman went to South Carolina, where she acted as a nurse, cook, scout, and spy for the Union army. After the war she raised money for black schools and opened a home for elderly blacks.

Tubman was small in stature—only about five feet tall—but enormous in courage and faith. "I said to the Lord, I'm going to hold steady on to you, and I know you'll see me through," she said. Because of her determination to lead others to freedom, she came to be known by a name of old: Moses.

WE ARE ALL
DESCENDANTS OF 1776

O n July 10, 1858, during his campaign for the US Senate, Abraham Lincoln gave a speech in Chicago, in which he reflected on the Declaration of Independence:

It happens that we meet together once every year, sometime about the 4th of July. . . . We run our memory back over the pages of history [to 1776]. We find a race of men living in that day whom we claim as our fathers and grandfathers. They were iron men. They fought for the principle that they were contending for; and we understand that by what they then did, it has followed that the degree of prosperity that we now enjoy has come to us. We hold this annual celebration to remind ourselves of all the good done, of how it was done and who did it, and how we are historically connected with it. . . .

We have [among us immigrants] who are not descendants at all of these men. . . . If they look back through this history to trace their connection with those days by blood, they find they have none. . . . But when they look through that old Declaration of Independence, they find that those old men say that "We hold these truths to be self-evident, that all men are created equal." And then they feel that that moral sentiment taught in that day evidences their relation to those men, that it is the father of all moral principle in them, and that they have a right to claim it as though they were blood of the blood, and flesh of the flesh of the men who wrote that Declaration. And so they are. That is the electric cord in that Declaration that links the hearts of patriotic and liberty-loving men together, that will link those patriotic hearts as long as the love of freedom exists in the minds of men throughout the world.

SAM HOUSTON

*S*am Houston lived a life as big as Texas. Born in Virginia, he moved to the Tennessee frontier with his family at age thirteen and soon struck out on his own. He lived for a while with the Cherokee, taught in a one-room schoolhouse, fought the Creek Indians under Andrew Jackson, studied law and was elected to Congress, became governor of Tennessee, became the first president of the Republic of Texas, represented Texas in the US Senate, and served as governor of Texas.

His finest moment came toward the end of his life, as the Civil War approached, and a secession convention voted to take Texas out of the Union. Houston opposed the move with every fiber of his soul. He took to the hustings to warn scornful crowds that secession would bring only disaster. In one town, when an armed man threatened him, the sixty-eight-year-old Houston stared him down, declaring, "Ladies and gentlemen, keep your seats. It is nothing but a fice [a small dog] barking at the lion in his den."

His efforts weren't enough. Texas legislators demanded that Governor Houston swear loyalty to the Confederacy. "In the name of my own conscience and manhood . . . I refuse to take this oath," he wrote, knowing it meant the end of his career.

Supporters offered to take up arms to fight for control of the statehouse, but Houston turned them down. He did not want to cling to office by spilling the blood of fellow Texans. Brokenhearted, he retired to private life. It was for this final act of public service that John F. Kennedy would later make Sam Houston a hero in his book *Profiles in Courage*.

THE BATTLE HYMN OF
THE REPUBLIC

Julia Ward Howe, a writer, lecturer, and antislavery reformer, was visiting a Union army camp during the Civil War when she heard soldiers singing the song "John Brown's Body," which began with the words "John Brown's body lies a-moldering in the grave." A clergyman with her suggested she write new lyrics to the tune. As she told it:

> I went to bed and slept as usual, but awoke the next morning in the gray of the early dawn, and to my astonishment found that the wished-for lines were arranging themselves in my brain. I lay quite still until the last verse had completed itself in my thoughts, then hastily arose . . . searched for an old sheet of paper and an old stub of a pen which I had had the night before, and began to scrawl the lines almost without looking.

Howe submitted her verses—which began "Mine eyes have seen the glory of the coming of the Lord: He is trampling out the vintage where the grapes of wrath are stored"—to the *Atlantic Monthly*, which accepted them and paid her a fee of four dollars. The magazine printed the lyrics on the first page of its February 1862 issue under the title "Battle Hymn of the Republic."

The song quickly became a favorite of the Union army. In the decades since, in times of war and peace, it has remained one of America's most-loved hymns.

YOUR SOLDIER BOY

In the summer of 1862, Civil War casualties poured into Washington, DC. Day after day, steamers carrying injured soldiers arrived. Makeshift hospitals sprang up throughout the capital in churches, government buildings, hotels, and private homes. The First Lady, Mary Todd Lincoln, formed the habit of visiting the wounded. Arriving with a carriage full of fruit and fresh flowers, she spent hours sitting at their bedsides, talking and reading to them, trying to make them more comfortable.

Often she helped them write letters home. "I am sitting by the side of your soldier boy," she wrote in one. "He has been quite sick and is getting well. He tells me to say that he is all right." She signed the letter, "With respect [for] the mother of a young soldier."

The Washington newspapers often criticized her for her receptions and decorating projects at the White House. One of the president's assistants believed she should publicize her hospital visits. "If she were worldly wise she would carry newspaper correspondents every time she went," he observed.

But the First Lady kept her hospital visits discreet and let the newspapers lavish praise on society women more press-savvy in their charity work. Her attempts to comfort the wounded were too profound to be a public relations tool. "She found something more gratifying than public acknowledgment," notes historian Doris Kearns Goodwin. "For in the hours she spent with these soldiers she must have sensed their unwavering belief in her husband and in the Union for which they fought. Such a faith was not readily found elsewhere—not in the cabinet, the Congress, the press, or the social circles of the city."

LEE AT GETTYSBURG

The incident below, related by a Union army veteran in A. L. Long's *Memoirs of Robert E. Lee*, is said to have taken place on July 3, 1863, the last day of the Battle of Gettysburg. It speaks of an American brotherhood that, in the end, transcended that terrible war.

I was at the battle of Gettysburg myself. . . . I had been a most bitter anti-South man, and fought and cursed the Confederates desperately. I could see nothing good in any of them. The last day of the fight a ball shattered my left leg. I lay on the ground, and as General Lee ordered his retreat he and his officers rode near me.

As they came along I recognized him, and, though faint from exposure and loss of blood, I raised up my hands, looked Lee in the face, and shouted as loud as I could, "Hurrah for the Union!"

The general heard me, looked, stopped his horse, dismounted, and came toward me. I confess that I at first thought he meant to kill me. But as he came up he looked down at me with such a sad expression upon his face that all fear left me, and I wondered what he was about. He extended his hand to me, and grasping mine firmly and looking right into my eyes, said, "My son, I hope you will soon be well."

If I live to be a thousand years I shall never forget the expression on General Lee's face. There he was, defeated, retiring from a field that had cost him and his cause almost their last hope, yet he stopped to say words like those to a wounded soldier of the opposition who had taunted him as he passed by. As soon as the general had left me I cried myself to sleep there upon the bloody ground.

MARY EDWARDS WALKER

September 20, 1863, brought the end of the Battle of Chickamauga in northwest Georgia, some of the hardest fighting of the Civil War. As Union casualties streamed into Chattanooga, Tennessee, many soldiers were surprised to find that the doctor tending their wounds was a woman dressed in gold-striped trousers, a green surgeon's sash, and a straw hat with an ostrich feather.

Mary Edwards Walker had graduated from Syracuse Medical College eight years earlier, becoming one of America's first female doctors. That was unusual enough, but Walker set herself even further apart by refusing to wear long, heavy dresses, opting instead for pants. She was born to break molds. When the Civil War began, she volunteered to serve as a doctor. The army wasn't sure what to make of her, but doctors were in short supply, and she was soon working near Union lines as a volunteer field surgeon. She requested a commission as an officer but was turned down since she was a woman. She went on volunteering, treating both soldiers and civilians.

After the war the army awarded Dr. Walker the Medal of Honor in recognition of her service. To Walker, the medal represented the recognition she had so long wanted. She was outraged when, in 1916, the army decided to rescind more than nine hundred medals as undeserved— including hers, because she had never officially been in the army. Walker refused to return her award. On the contrary, she proudly wore it every day for the rest of her life.

In 1977 the army restored Mary Edwards Walker's medal on the grounds that, had she been a man, she would have been commissioned as an officer. She remains the sole female recipient of the Medal of Honor.

FULL SPEED AHEAD

*A*ugust 5, 1864, saw the last major naval battle of the Civil War when Admiral David Glasgow Farragut led a fleet of Union ships against Mobile Bay, Alabama, one of the most heavily defended ports in the South. The entrance to the bay was protected by Fort Morgan and Fort Gaines, four Confederate ships, including the giant ironclad *Tennessee*, and dozens of mines, which in those days were called "torpedoes." The Confederates had arranged the mines, which lurked just beneath the water's surface, to create a narrow channel running into the bay.

As the attack began, Farragut climbed into the rigging of his flagship, the *Hartford*, to get a good view. There he watched in dismay as one of his ships, the ironclad *Tecumseh*, steered into the minefield and hit a torpedo. An explosion erupted beneath its waterline. The *Tecumseh* lurched to one side, stopped dead in the water, and a few minutes later went straight to the bottom, taking more than ninety men to their deaths.

At once the rest of the fleet faltered and began to drift toward Fort Morgan. The Confederate gunners raked the Union vessels with deadly fire. Farragut knew that to hesitate would mean disaster, and he shouted his famous order: "Damn the torpedoes! Full speed ahead!"

Farragut's ship steamed forward, straight through the minefield. The horrified sailors heard the mine cases thudding against the hull, but none exploded. The other ships followed, and soon Mobile Bay was in Union hands. Farragut's exclamation has become a rallying cry for Americans in times that call for meeting danger head-on.

JANE ADDAMS

*D*emocratic government, associated as it is with all the mistakes and shortcomings of the common people, still remains the most valuable contribution America has made to the moral life of the world," wrote Jane Addams, born September 6, 1860, in Cedarville, Illinois. She heightened that contribution with Hull House, a "settlement house" in Chicago where Addams and other reformers helped the poor, including immigrant families.

As Addams recounted in her book *Twenty Years at Hull House*, the seeds of her passion were planted at about age seven on a day when she passed through the poorest part of a neighboring town with her father, a prosperous miller.

> On that day I had my first sight of the poverty which implies squalor, and felt the curious distinction between the ruddy poverty of the country and that which even a small city presents in its shabbiest streets. I remember launching at my father the pertinent inquiry why people lived in such horrid little houses so close together, and that after receiving his explanation I declared with much firmness when I grew up I should, of course, have a large house, but it would not be built among the other large houses, but right in the midst of horrid little houses like these.

More than two decades later, Addams moved into a dilapidated Chicago mansion once owned by businessman Charles J. Hull. There in the crowded immigrant slums, she and her fellow reformers provided shelter, education, and affection for thousands—everything from maternal care and concerts to language classes and lessons in citizenship. Addams served as head resident of Hull House for forty-six years—the rest of her life—practicing a democracy that welcomed "the common people" from around the world.

JOHN WESLEY POWELL:
INTO THE UNKNOWN

*I*n the mid-nineteenth century, much of the Southwest was unknown territory—a blank space on US maps labeled "Unexplored." Reports from a few hunters and Native Americans told of an enormous canyon carved by the Colorado River. In 1869 geologist John Wesley Powell set out to find the canyon and ride the river between its walls.

Powell started on the Green River with four boats and a handful of companions. They got a hint of what was to come when foaming torrents tossed one of the boats against a boulder and dashed it to pieces.

Several days later, Powell—who had lost an arm in the Civil War—decided to climb a cliff to get a view of the water's current. Eighty feet up, he found himself clinging to a rock with no good foothold, and nowhere to go. His climbing partner took off his pants and lowered them to Powell, who made a life-or-death lunge for the waving cloth, grabbed hold, and scrambled to safety.

The explorers floated into the Colorado River and its huge canyon. Three-thousand-foot walls loomed overhead. Traveling west, they passed carved arches and spires. At times they battled whirlpools and craggy falls. They ran short on food and supplies. Then they came upon a stretch of monstrous rapids.

Three of the men decided to climb out of the canyon and walk back to civilization. They were never seen again.

The rest decided to take two boats and run the terrifying rapids. They dashed into the boiling tide, disappeared in the foam—and then reappeared, the men still clinging on.

On August 29, 1869, three months and a thousand miles after they started, the boats floated into open country. Powell had accomplished one of the most storied journeys in American exploration: the first expedition through the Grand Canyon.

SUSAN B. ANTHONY

Susan B. Anthony was born on February 15, 1820, in an age when women in the United States and the rest of the world were considered inferior to men. Most colleges weren't open to women. Many restaurants had signs saying "No Females Allowed." Husbands by law controlled their wives' property and any money they might earn. Women could not hold most jobs and public offices, or even vote.

Anthony spent most of her life trying to right those injustices. She founded women's rights groups and wrote books, pamphlets, and articles. She crossed the country again and again to give speeches in town halls, schoolhouses, barns, sawmills, log cabins—anyplace where people would listen. Crowds sometimes shouted her down or pelted her with rotten eggs. Newspapers called her names. Mobs burned her effigies. But Anthony would not give up.

On Election Day 1872, she showed up at a poll in Rochester, New York, and cast a vote for president. Two weeks later, a marshal knocked on her door with a warrant for her arrest. At trial the judge prohibited her from speaking on her own behalf and ordered the jury to find her guilty of voting illegally. The court fined Anthony one hundred dollars. "I will never pay a dollar of your unjust penalty," she replied. And she didn't.

Anthony died in 1906. Fourteen years later, the Nineteenth Amendment to the Constitution finally gave women the right to vote.

Today the US is a world leader in women's rights. In no other country do women enjoy more freedom and opportunity. And in the struggle for equal rights, no name deserves more honor than that of Susan B. Anthony.

BUFFALO BILL

The name William Frederick Cody, born in 1846 in Scott County, Iowa, may not ring a bell. But chances are you know Cody's nickname, Buffalo Bill.

Cody left home at age eleven, after his father died, and cut a fearless path across the Western frontier. Cowboy, teamster, fur trapper, gold miner, Pony Express rider, Civil War soldier, cavalry scout, Indian fighter—he did it all. He earned his nickname while hunting buffalo to supply meat for railroad work crews—reportedly killing more than four thousand buffalo in eighteen months. A few years later, when he served as a scout for army troops, and the government awarded him the Congressional Medal of Honor for valor in action.

In 1872 Cody decided to take advantage of his growing fame and began a long career as a showman. His "Buffalo Bill's Wild West" spectacular toured the country with hundreds of cowboys, cowgirls, and Native Americans—including sure-shot Annie Oakley and Sitting Bull—as well as live buffalo and cattle. The show's mock shoot-outs and round-ups thrilled audiences. Cody even toured Europe and performed for the queen of England. "Buffalo Bill has come, we have seen, and he has conquered," a British newspaper reported. By the turn of the twentieth century, Cody was perhaps the most famous American of his day.

Buffalo Bill was, in some ways, a man of contradictions. He hunted buffalo, but later supported their conservation. He loved the frontier, but in promoting it helped it disappear. "The West of the old times, with its strong characters, its stern battles and its tremendous stretches of loneliness, can never be blotted from my mind," he wrote. "Nor can it, I hope, be blotted from the memory of the American people."

ANNIE OAKLEY

Sharpshooter Annie Oakley was born Phoebe Ann Moses in 1860 in a cabin in Darke County, Ohio. She took her first shot at age eight ("one of the best shots I ever made," she later said) and soon began shooting rabbits to help feed her destitute family. Around age fifteen she started shooting game for a nearby grocer, who sold it to hotels. She earned enough to pay off the mortgage on her widowed mother's house.

When expert marksman Frank Butler passed through the area, Annie entered a shooting match against him. "I almost dropped dead when a little slim girl in short dresses stepped out to the mark with me," Butler recalled. They each shot at twenty-five pigeons. Butler hit 24; Annie hit all 25. "Right then and there I decided if I could get that girl I would do it," Butler said. They courted and married. She adopted the stage name Annie Oakley, and they performed together in shooting exhibitions.

Buffalo Bill hired them for his Wild West show. Crowds lined up to see her shoot the flame off a distant candle, or the heart in the ace of hearts. She shot apples from her husband's head and the ashes off cigarettes in his mouth. Sometimes she shot backward looking into a mirror.

The Sioux chief Sitting Bull called her "Little Sure Shot" and admired her so much that he adopted her. When touring in Europe, Germany's crown prince (the future Kaiser Wilhelm) invited her to shoot a cigarette out of his mouth. She demurred but did shoot a cigarette out of his hand.

The Broadway musical *Annie Get Your Gun*, with songs by Irving Berlin, is based on Annie Oakley's life. Will Rogers called her the "greatest rifle shot the world has ever produced. Nobody took her place. There was only one."

MR. WATSON, COME HERE

*A*lexander Graham Bell had two great passions: helping the deaf and inventing. He was born in 1847 in Scotland, where his father taught the art of public speaking and helped deaf people learn to speak. When Alexander was a young man, his family immigrated to Canada, and he soon moved south to Boston, Massachusetts, where he opened a school for teachers of the deaf.

In Boston, Bell grew fascinated with the idea of developing a way to send voices over telegraph wires. He became fast friends with a young mechanic named Thomas Watson, who helped him with his experiments.

For months, the two tinkered with electric currents, switches, and reeds. March 10, 1876, brought one of the great moments in the history of invention. Bell was hard at work in his laboratory, preparing to test a new transmitter he had recently designed, when he spilled some battery acid on his clothes. "Mr. Watson, come here! I want you!" he called. Watson rushed from another room to Bell's side, not with alarm, but with excitement. He had heard Bell's call on their instrument. It was the first time words had ever traveled over a wire. Alexander Graham Bell had just given the world the telephone.

The next year, the young inventor launched the Bell Telephone Company, which grew into one of the world's largest corporations. But Bell had little interest in business. He spent the rest of his life coming up with new ideas and finding ways to help the deaf. He became a proud US citizen in 1882 and is still remembered as one of America's greatest inventors.

LAURA INGALLS WILDER

*L*aura Ingalls Wilder was born in 1867 in an area then known as the "Big Woods" of western Wisconsin. "I was born in a log house within four miles of the legend-haunted Lake Pippin in Wisconsin," she wrote. "I remember seeing deer that my father had killed, hanging in the trees about our forest home. When I was four years old we traveled to the Indian Territory. My childish memories hold the sound of the war whoop and I see pictures of painted Indians.

"I was a regular little tomboy, and it was fun to walk the two miles to school," she recalled, although she also confessed, "My education has been what a girl would get on the frontier. . . . I never graduated from anything and only attended high school two terms." After moves to Minnesota and Iowa, Laura's family established a homestead claim near De Smet, South Dakota, where she grew up and married Almanzo Wilder. "It was there I learned to do all kinds of farm work with machinery," she recalled. "I have ridden the binder, driving six horses. And I could ride. I do not wish to appear conceited, but I broke my own ponies to ride. Of course they were not bad but they were broncos. . . . And, believe me, I learned how to take care of hens and make them lay."

Later, in Mansfield, Missouri, Laura began writing down memories of her pioneer life. During the Great Depression, she asked her daughter Rose, a writer, to look at her manuscript, written in pencil on lined school tablets. Rose helped her turn portions into a novel, and in 1932, when Laura Ingalls Wilder was sixty-five years old, *Little House in the Big Woods* was published. *Little House on the Prairie* and other books followed, turning the former pioneer into one of America's most beloved authors.

THE GREATEST INVENTOR
OF THEM ALL

The story of Thomas Edison, born in 1847 in Milan, Ohio, is the stuff the American dream is made of. He dropped out of school when his teacher called him "addled," so his mother taught him at home, where he set up a chemical laboratory in his basement. Soon he was on his way to becoming the greatest inventor the world has known.

As a young man, Edison built an "invention factory" in New Jersey. It became America's first research laboratory for industry. He amazed a group of onlookers one day when he recited "Mary Had a Little Lamb" into a device and then turned a crank to make his voice come back out. Edison had invented the phonograph, the first machine for recording sounds. On October 21, 1879, he gave the world the invention for which he is best known—the electric lightbulb.

Edison worked eighteen hours a day and never feared failure. Once, he conducted experiment after experiment without getting the results he needed, and a friend said he was sorry the tests were failing. "Shucks, we haven't failed," Edison said. "Now we know a thousand things that won't work, so we're that much closer to finding what will."

One night in 1914 a tremendous fire destroyed his factories in West Orange, New Jersey. "We'll build bigger and better on the ruins," the sixty-seven-year-old inventor declared. And he did.

Thomas Edison patented more than one thousand inventions. He created new kinds of batteries, improved the telephone, invented a motion-picture machine, and helped found one of America's most famous industries: the movies.

Throughout his long career, Edison always insisted that hard work was the main reason for his success. "Genius is 1 percent inspiration, and 99 percent perspiration," he said. Americans have built a great nation by following that rule.

ANGEL OF THE BATTLEFIELD

*W*hen the Civil War broke out, former schoolteacher Clara Barton begged Union generals to let her go to the front lines to help the wounded. "A battlefield is no place for a woman," they told her. Barton hounded them until they gave in. Loading a wagon with supplies, she headed to the front and nursed injured men as shells whistled overhead.

At the Battle of Antietam, a bullet tore through the sleeve of her dress, killing the wounded soldier she was tending. She kept risking her life at front lines across the South, from Fredericksburg to Charleston. The grateful soldiers began to call her the Angel of the Battlefield.

After the war she directed a search for missing men and helped mark the graves of nearly 13,000 Union soldiers who died at the Andersonville Prison in Georgia. On a trip to Europe, she helped organize the relief efforts of the International Red Cross in the Franco-Prussian War.

A decade later, on May 21, 1881, Barton founded the American Red Cross. For the next two decades, she was on the scene, delivering relief in times of natural disaster and war, including the Johnstown Flood of 1889, the 1898 explosion of the USS *Maine* ("I am with the wounded," she wrote to President McKinley from Cuba), and the Great Galveston Hurricane of 1900. She helped provide relief for victims of famine and war in Russia, the Balkans, Armenia, and Cuba.

Barton served as president of the American Red Cross until age eighty-two. She died in 1912, eight years after her retirement. Her own words sum up her drive to aid others: "The door that nobody else will go in at, seems always to swing open widely for me."

GRANT'S MEMOIRS

*I*n 1884 Ulysses S. Grant, former general of the Union armies and president of the United States, suddenly found himself penniless and humiliated. His brokerage firm, Grant and Ward, had collapsed with the discovery that his partner, Ferdinand Ward, was a crook who had stolen investors' money. Sixty-two-year-old Grant, an honorable and beloved man, was devastated.

And it got worse. That fall he consulted a doctor about a nagging soreness in his throat. The expression on the specialist's face told Grant the news was bad. "Is it cancer?" he asked. It was, and there was little hope of survival.

Grant quickly made a decision. He had never wanted to write his memoirs, but he realized that would be the best way to provide for his wife, Julia, and his family. If the book sold well, they would have some financial security when he was gone. His friend Mark Twain agreed to publish the work.

So Grant started writing, in a race against death. "My family is American, and has been for generations, in all its branches, direct and collateral," he began. The Grants moved to the Adirondack Mountains, hoping the mountain air would make him more comfortable. Every day he sat on the porch, propped in a chair, barely able even to swallow, suffering from intense pain in his throat, but writing steadily.

He wrote mainly of his military career, but also of his confidence that Northerners and Southerners would once again be fast friends. "I cannot stay to be a living witness to the correctness of this prophecy," he wrote, "but I feel it within me that it is to be so."

Grant finished the manuscript on July 18, 1885. Five days later, on July 23, he died. *The Personal Memoirs of Ulysses S. Grant* was a huge best seller, providing large royalties for the general's widow. Written in clear, unadorned prose, it remains a classic of American literature.

A DARING ADVENTURE

*E*arly 1887 brought a profound change to six-year-old Helen Keller's life when a young teacher named Anne Sullivan arrived at her house in Alabama. Together, the girl and her teacher would inspire the world.

Helen was not two years old when she came down with an illness that robbed her of sight and hearing for the rest of her life. For the next few years she grew up, as she later wrote, "wild and unruly, giggling and chuckling to express pleasure; kicking, scratching, uttering the choked screams of the deaf-mute to indicate the opposite."

Then Anne Sullivan arrived from Boston and moved in with Helen's family, determined to help the girl break out of her lonely world of darkness and silence. With painstaking determination and love, Anne taught Helen to spell words with her fingers, then to read and write braille. Eventually, Helen learned to speak. Anne devoted much of the rest of her life to her student. With her help, Helen grew up to:

- graduate from prestigious Radcliffe College with honors;
- give lectures around the globe and write books that sold the world over;
- star in a movie about her own life;
- meet with every president from Grover Cleveland to Lyndon Johnson;
- receive countless awards, from France's Legion of Honor to the US Presidential Medal of Freedom; and

- swim, ride horses and bicycles, play chess, go camping, and ride in an open-cockpit airplane.

Americans loved Helen Keller for her unconquerable spirit. "Life," she once wrote, "is either a daring adventure or nothing."

AROUND THE WORLD IN
SEVENTY-TWO DAYS

*I*n 1873, the French novelist Jules Verne published *Around the World in Eighty Days*, in which Englishman Phileas Fogg wins a bet that he can circle the world in eighty days. Sixteen years later, intrepid *New York World* reporter Nellie Bly decided to beat Fogg's fictional trip, something never done before.

On November 14, 1889, carrying a crocodile gripsack, she boarded the *Augusta Victoria* and steamed across the Atlantic. Reaching England, she made a quick detour to France to meet Verne himself. "Good luck, Nellie Bly," he toasted her. Then it was on by mail train to Brindisi, Italy, where she sent a hurried cable to her editors before sailing for the Suez Canal.

The *World* published daily reports on its feminine Phileas Fogg's progress. "Can Jules Verne's great dream be reduced to actual fact?" it asked. The whole country followed the attempt to "girdle the spinning globe."

Nellie raced on. On the boat to Egypt, two men proposed marriage. In Ceylon she impatiently waited five days for a ship. In Singapore she bought a monkey. En route to Hong Kong, a monsoon filled passengers' cabins with water. Another storm hit as she steamed across the Pacific. The ship's crew posted a sign: "For Nellie Bly, We'll win or die!"

Nearing San Francisco, she heard rumors of a smallpox quarantine onboard ship. She jumped on a tugboat and headed for land. Blizzards had stranded locomotives in the mountains, so she hopped on a train taking a southern route and dashed across the continent.

On January 25, 1890, cannons boomed and crowds cheered as Nellie arrived in Jersey City. She looked at her watch: 72 days 6 hours 11 minutes—she'd beaten Phileas Fogg by a week. "Father Time Outdone!" the *World* trumpeted. Around the globe, young Nellie Bly became a symbol of the American can-do spirit.

MARK TWAIN ON
FOREIGN CRITICS

$\mathcal{M}$ark Twain, born November 30, 1835, was a loving critic of his country, usually with humor. ("There is no distinctly native American criminal class except Congress," he once observed.) But disdain for America by European snobs raised his hackles. In an 1890 address in Boston, he let loose.

If I look harried and worn, it is not from an ill conscience. It is from sitting up nights to worry about the foreign critic. He won't concede that we have a civilization—a "real" civilization. . . . [H]e said we had never contributed anything to the betterment of the world. . . .

What is a "real" civilization? [Let us suppose it is one without despotic government and near-universal inequality, ignorance, and poverty. In that case] there are some partial civilizations scattered around Europe—pretty lofty civilizations they are, but who begot them? What is the seed from which they sprang? Liberty and intelligence. What planted that seed? There are dates and statistics which suggest that it was the American Revolution that planted it. When that revolution began, monarchy had been on trial some thousands of years, over there, and was a distinct and convicted failure. . . . [W]e hoisted the banner of revolution and raised the first genuine shout for human liberty that had ever been heard. . . .

Who summoned the French slaves to rise and set the nation free?

We did it. What resulted in England and on the Continent? Crippled liberty took up its bed and walked. From that day to this its march has not halted, and please God it never will. We are called the nation of inventors. And we are. We could still claim that title and wear its loftiest honors, if we had stopped with the first thing we ever invented—which was human liberty. . . . *We* have contributed nothing! Nothing hurts me like ingratitude.

THE ORIGINS OF BASKETBALL

*J*ames Naismith, an instructor at the YMCA's School for Christian Workers in Springfield, Massachusetts, received a tough assignment in December 1891. The head of the school's physical education department gave him two weeks to come up with a new game that young men could play indoors during the cold winter months.

He tinkered with different ideas for several days, and then he remembered a game from his childhood called "duck on a rock," in which players tried to knock a small rock off a big rock by throwing stones at it. The memory of stones arching through the air at a target gave him just the inspiration he needed. He had the school custodian nail two peach baskets to the railing of a ten-foot-high balcony that ran around the school gymnasium. Since his class had eighteen students, he divided them into two teams of nine and explained that players scored by throwing a soccer ball into a basket.

"The first words were not very encouraging when one of the class made the remark, 'Humph, a new game,'" Naismith later said. "I asked the boys to try it once as a favor to me. They started, and after the ball was first thrown up there was no need of further coaxing."

The game was an instant hit. But it needed a name. One student suggested Naismithball, which the sport's inventor rejected. Then someone came up with "basketball"—since, after all, players threw the ball into peach baskets. In the early days the baskets had no holes in the bottoms, so someone had to climb up and get the ball out whenever anyone scored.

Basketball is now America's most popular indoor sport. James Naismith, who was born in Ontario, Canada, became a proud US citizen in 1925.

PRESIDENTIAL TRIVIA

$\mathcal{W}$ hich president served two nonconsecutive terms? Hint: He was elected in 1884 and again in 1892, with Benjamin Harrison serving as president between his two terms. Answer below.

Which presidents signed the Declaration of Independence?
John Adams, Thomas Jefferson

Which presidents signed the Constitution?
George Washington, James Madison

Which president served the shortest time in office?
William H. Harrison, 31 days

Which president served the longest?
Franklin D. Roosevelt, 12 years, 39 days

Who was the youngest person to be elected president?
John F. Kennedy, 43

Who was the youngest person to become president?
Theodore Roosevelt, 42*

Who was the oldest person to become president?
Joe Biden, 78

Who was the only president to resign?
Richard Nixon

Which presidents were impeached?

Andrew Johnson, Bill Clinton, Donald Trump

Which president served two non-consecutive terms?
  Grover Cleveland

Which president was never elected either as president or vice president?
  Gerald Ford

* Theodore Roosevelt was forty-two in 1901 when he succeeded McKinley, who had been assassinated. John F. Kennedy was forty-three when elected president in 1960.

THE MAN WHO GAVE BACK

*A*ndrew Carnegie emigrated from Scotland to America in 1848 when he was twelve years old. He found a job in a Pittsburgh cotton mill, working twelve-hour days for $1.20 a week. He spent his spare time educating himself in a local library and soon managed to get a better job as a messenger, then a telegraph operator.

Eventually his hard work caught the eye of a Pennsylvania Railroad official, who hired the young man as a clerk. After that, Carnegie's rise was rapid. Realizing that the growing United States would need lots of steel, he opened a steel plant in 1875. Over the next quarter century he built a business empire. On March 24, 1900, he incorporated his Carnegie Steel Company, and then turned around and sold it a year later, a transaction that made him one of the richest men in the world.

The most interesting part was still to come. Carnegie had made up his mind that he would not die rich. He had the idea that a person should spend the first part of life making money, and the second part giving it away. "The man who dies rich, dies disgraced," he said.

He spent the rest of his years giving away his money. Starting public libraries was his special love. Reading books had opened the way for him, and he wanted others to have the same chance. He started more than 2,500 libraries around the world—a gift that has touched millions of lives. By the time he died at age eighty-three, Carnegie had given away the vast majority of his riches to charities.

Carnegie's career had its blemishes. While he earned millions, unskilled laborers in his mills worked for fourteen cents an hour. Yet in the end, he made his mark not by how much he made but by how much he gave back.

THE MAN IN THE ARENA

*A*t 2:15 a.m. on September 14, 1901, President William McKinley died in Buffalo, New York, from wounds left by an assassin's bullet. On the same day, Theodore Roosevelt stood in the library of a friend's house in Buffalo and took the oath of office to become the twenty-sixth president of the United States. At age forty-two, he was the youngest man ever to assume the office.

"It is a dreadful thing to come into the presidency in this way," Roosevelt observed. Yet he woke the next morning ready to stride into the arena of history. A friend once said that Roosevelt was a many-sided man and "every side was like an electric battery."

Cowboy, explorer, naturalist, Rough Rider, author, politician—he was just the dynamo the young United States needed for a new century. Several years later, in a speech on "Citizenship in a Republic," Teddy Roosevelt described his approach to governing and to life:

> It is not the critic who counts: not the man who points out how the strong man stumbles or where the doer of deeds could have done better. The credit belongs to the man who is actually in the arena, whose face is marred by dust and sweat and blood, who strives valiantly, who errs and comes up short again and again, because there is no effort without error or shortcoming, but who knows the great enthusiasms, the great devotions, who spends himself for a worthy cause; who, at the best, knows, in the end, the triumph of high achievement, and who, at the worst, if he fails, at least he fails while daring greatly, so that his place shall never be with those cold and timid souls who knew neither victory nor defeat.

THE PRESIDENT AND
THE TEDDY BEAR

*M*illions of children cuddle up with their favorite teddy bears. How did toy bears come to be so popular, and how did they come to be called "teddy"? Credit Teddy Roosevelt, as well as a political cartoonist and some resourceful entrepreneurs.

In 1902 Roosevelt, an avid outdoorsman, went on a bear-hunting trip in Mississippi. The president was a good hunter, but on this particular trip, he had terrible luck. For several days, he never even saw a bear.

Finally one of his guides cornered a small black bear, wounded it, and tied it to a tree. Then he called for the president to come shoot it. Teddy the sportsman resolutely refused. He had eagerly shot grizzly bears in the Wild West, but he had no interest in taking unfair advantage of a terrified, trapped animal.

When *Washington Post* cartoonist Clifford Berryman heard the story, he drew a picture of the president turning away in disgust from the idea of shooting the helpless bear. The nation loved the fact that their president had spared the poor creature, and in no time it became the story of "Teddy's bear."

By early 1903, two Russian Jewish immigrants named Morris and Rose Michtom were making and selling stuffed "Teddy bears" in their Brooklyn shop. About the same time, toy company FAO Schwarz of New York City began selling plush teddy bears made in a German toy factory. A worldwide craze began, which shows no sign of ebbing more than a century later.

A FEW PRESIDENTIAL FIRSTS

*O*n August 22, 1902, Theodore Roosevelt became the first US president to ride in a car in public when he rolled through the streets of Hartford, Connecticut, in a purple-lined Columbia Electric Victoria, followed by a twenty-carriage procession. The *New York Times* reported that "two expert New York chauffeurs" had charge of the automobile. "The President expressed his satisfaction at the substitution of drives for conventional handshaking," the paper said. "This method of entertainment seems to have given the people the opportunity desired of seeing him."

A few more presidential firsts:

Who was the first president to ride a train while in office?
Andrew Jackson, June 6, 1833

Who was the first president to be photographed in office?
James Polk, February 14, 1849

Who was the first president to have a White House telephone?
Rutherford B. Hayes, 1879

Who was the first president to have electricity in the White House?
Benjamin Harrison, 1891

Who was the first president to make a radio broadcast?
Warren G. Harding, June 14, 1922

Who was the first president to appear on TV?
Franklin D. Roosevelt, at the New York World's Fair, New York City, April 30, 1939

Who was the first president to fly in an airplane while in office?

Franklin D. Roosevelt, January 1943, to the Casablanca Conference with Winston Churchill

Who was the first president to hold a press conference filmed for TV?

Dwight D. Eisenhower, January 19, 1955

Who was the first president to fly in a helicopter?

Dwight D. Eisenhower, July 12, 1957

Who was the first president to hold a live televised press conference?

John F. Kennedy, January 25, 1961

A HORSELESS CARRIAGE

*T*hirty-one-year-old Horatio Nelson Jackson was visiting San Francisco's University Club in 1903 when someone wagered fifty dollars that it would be impossible to drive an automobile to New York in less than ninety days. Jackson immediately took the bet. He did not own an auto, and no one had ever crossed the continent by car. At that time, the United States boasted only 150 miles of paved roads—all of them inside cities. "Highways" were often nothing more than two ruts leading toward the horizon.

Jackson purchased a used, twenty-horsepower car made by the Winton Motor Carriage Company of Cleveland, christened it the *Vermont* after his home state, and hired mechanic Sewall Crocker to accompany him. They loaded the auto with supplies, and on May 23, 1903, the two men left San Francisco on the first drive "from sea to sea in a horseless carriage," as the *San Francisco Examiner* reported.

They bounced along cliffside ledges, splashed across bridgeless streams, zigzagged over trackless plains. Tires blew out, springs broke, bolts sheared off, parts rattled to pieces. Bad directions took them hundreds of miles out of the way. They lost count of how many times they had to haul the *Vermont* out of mud holes. But at every farm, village, and town, curious folks gave them a hand. Blacksmiths helped them make repairs. In Idaho they bought a bulldog named Bud, fitted him with driving goggles, and took him along for the rest of the ride.

On July 26, the mud-covered *Vermont* rolled into Manhattan. The journey had taken sixty-three days. Though he never bothered to collect his fifty dollars, Horatio Nelson Jackson won his bet. The age of the open road had dawned for the American automobile.

THE US MILITARY RESERVE

O n April 23, 1908, President Theodore Roosevelt created a new component within the US Army—the Medical Reserve Corps. In an age when disease and infection killed more soldiers than battle wounds, the new corps of 360 medical professionals stood ready to become active-duty officers with the army in times of conflict.

That corps was the beginning of the US military's federal reserve force. During the next several years, the army created additional reserve corps to fight and perform other duties when needed.

Today hundreds of thousands of Americans serve in the federal military reserve for the Army, Navy, Air Force, Marines, and Coast Guard. These ready-to-go civilians put on uniforms once a month or more to train and help maintain day-to-day operations for the military. The president can call them to active service anytime to help meet a national emergency.

US military reserve troops and National Guard troops perform very similar duties, and National Guard troops are also frequently referred to as "reserves." The main difference is that the US military reserve is controlled by the federal government. National Guard units answer to state governments, except when called into federal service by the president.

In many ways reservists form the backbone of the US military. Many are highly trained specialists who serve in roles that range from pilots to field doctors to logistics officers. When the nation goes to war, some of the most critical tasks are carried out by reservists. The United States could not engage in a major conflict without these men and women who are ready to go in harm's way for their country. To be a reservist, it is said, is to be twice a citizen.

MOTTOS AND WATCHWORDS
OF SOME WHO DEFEND US

*T*he various branches of the military and many military units have mottos that sum up their missions. The slogans speak volumes about the character of the men and women who serve in uniform. Here are a few of the mottos—some official, some unofficial—of those who defend us.

Army–This We'll Defend

Navy–*Non sibi sed patriae* (Not for self, but for country)

Air Force–Above All

Marine Corps–*Semper Fidelis* (Always Loyal)

Coast Guard–*Semper Paratus* (Always Prepared)

National Guard–Always ready, always there

US Military Academy (West Point)–Duty, Honor, Country

US Naval Academy–*Ex Scientia Tridens* (From Knowledge, Sea Power)

US Coast Guard Academy–*Scientiae Cedit Mare* (The sea yields to knowledge)

Green Berets–*De Oppresso Liber* (To liberate the oppressed)

Army Rangers–*Sua Sponte* (Of Their Own Accord) and Rangers Lead the Way

Army Corps of Engineers–*Essayons* (Let us try)

Navy SEALs–The only easy day was yesterday

Seabees–*Construimus, Batuimus* (We Build, We Fight) and Can Do!

THE BIRTH OF THE FBI

*D*uring President Theodore Roosevelt's administration, Attorney General Charles Bonaparte decided he needed a squad of investigators to handle a rising tide of crime and corruption. Bonaparte, grandnephew of Napoleon, appointed nine former Secret Service agents and twenty-five of his own men to form a special agent force. On July 26, 1908, he ordered the new force to begin conducting investigations for the Department of Justice. It was the birth of the Federal Bureau of Investigation—the FBI.

One of the agents' early assignments was to help stop the "white slave trade" that trafficked women into prostitution houses. After World War I, the relentless G-men (an abbreviation for "government men") began chasing down gangsters like John Dillinger, Al Capone, and "Baby Face" Nelson.

The FBI's famous Ten Most Wanted list began in 1950 after a reporter looking for story ideas asked the bureau for information about the ten "toughest guys" it would like to catch. The stories generated so much interest, the FBI decided to make the list permanent. More than 150 of the Ten Most Wanted Fugitives have been captured with the public's help.

Today the FBI numbers more than 35,000 special agents, analysts, scientists, and other personnel. They work around the globe, with headquarters in Washington, DC, fifty-six US field offices, and more than sixty international offices in US embassies. Agents investigate crimes ranging from civil rights violations to cyber-attacks. In recent years, they have helped prevent scores of terrorist attacks.

The list of FBI heroes is long. It includes men and women like Special Agent Leonard Hatton, a bomb specialist who was on his way to work in New York City on September 11, 2001, when he saw smoke rising from the World Trade Center. He ran to the scene to help others escape. When the towers collapsed, he died beneath them.

The motto of the FBI is "Fidelity, Bravery, Integrity."

A CITIZEN OF THE WORLD

*I*n April 1910 Theodore Roosevelt gave a speech in Paris in which he reflected on patriotism in a world that was just beginning to resemble what we today might call a "global village." A century later, his words are worth pondering.

I believe that a man must be a good patriot before he can be, and as the only possible way of being, a good citizen of the world. Experience teaches us that the average man who protests that his international feeling swamps his national feeling, that he does not care for his country because he cares so much for mankind, in actual practice proves himself the foe of mankind; that the man who says that he does not care to be a citizen of any one country, because he is a citizen of the world, is in very fact usually an exceedingly undesirable citizen of whatever corner of the world he happens at the moment to be in. . . . [I]f a man can view his own country and all other countries from the same level with tepid indifference, it is wise to distrust him, just as it is wise to distrust the man who can take the same dispassionate view of his wife and his mother. However broad and deep a man's sympathies, however intense his activities, he need have no fear that they will be cramped by love of his native land.

Now, this does not mean in the least that a man should not wish to do good outside of his native land. On the contrary, just as I think that the man who loves his family is more apt to be a good neighbor than the man who does not, so I think that the most useful member of the family of nations is normally a strongly patriotic nation.

AMERICA'S FIRST
LADY OF THE AIR

$\mathcal{H}$ arriet Quimby was already a journalist, theater critic, photographer, and screenwriter when she convinced an aviator to teach her to fly. In 1911, eight years after the Wright brothers' first flight, she became the first woman in the United States to earn a pilot's license. On April 16, 1912, she became the first woman to pilot a plane across the English Channel. Amelia Earhart later described Quimby's fragile craft as "hardly more than a winged skeleton with a motor." Quimby wrote about her flight from Dover to the French coast in *Leslie's Illustrated Weekly*:

> In a moment I was in the air, climbing steadily in a long circle. . . . In an instant I was beyond the cliffs and over the channel. . . . Then the quickening fog obscured my view. Calais was out of sight. I could not see ahead of me or at all below. There was only one thing for me to do and that was to keep my eyes fixed on my compass.
>
> My hands were covered with long Scotch woolen gloves which gave me good protection from the cold and fog; but the machine was wet and my face was so covered with dampness that I had to push my goggles up on my forehead. I could not see through them. I was traveling at over a mile a minute. The distance straight across from Dover to Calais is only twenty-five miles, and I knew that land must be in sight if I could only get below the fog and see it. So I dropped from an altitude of about two

thousand feet until I was half that height. The sunlight struck upon my face and my eyes lit upon the white and sandy shores of France.

Quimby's daring flight helped earn her the epithet "America's First Lady of the Air." Tragically, less than three months after her historic flight, she died in a flying accident near Boston.

UNCLE SAM

*P*eople all over the world recognize Uncle Sam—the tall, white-haired gentleman dressed in red, white, and blue—as a symbol of the United States. Where did this old fellow with the top hat come from?

No one knows for sure, but tradition says he first showed up during the War of 1812. Businessman Samuel Wilson of Troy, New York, who was known to friends as Uncle Sam, supplied the army with beef in barrels. The barrels were labeled "US" to show they belonged to the United States government. Somewhere along the way, it is said, folks began to joke that the "US" stood for Uncle Sam, and a national symbol was born.

Uncle Sam's stars-and-stripes costume originated in political cartoons of the nineteenth century. The best-known image first appeared on July 6, 1916, during World War I, on the cover of *Leslie's Weekly* magazine with the title "What Are You Doing for Preparedness?" The artist, James Montgomery Flagg, based his portrait of Uncle Sam on his own likeness to save the cost of hiring a model. The picture was so popular, the US government eventually turned it into the famous recruiting poster of Uncle Sam declaring, "I Want You."

ONE HERO'S PLEDGE

$\mathcal{M}$artin Treptow, a native of Chippewa Falls, Wisconsin, was working as a barber in Cherokee, Iowa, in 1917 when he enlisted in the army to fight in World War I. His regiment arrived in France in December of that year, and he wrote a pledge in his diary as a New Year's resolution for 1918. Ronald Reagan, in his first inaugural address, spoke of Treptow's fate:

> Under [a] marker lies a young man, Martin Treptow, who left his job in a small town barbershop in 1917 to go to France with the famed Rainbow Division. There, on the western front, he was killed trying to carry a message between battalions under heavy artillery fire.
>
> We're told that on his body was found a diary. On the flyleaf under the heading "My Pledge," he had written these words: "America must win this war. Therefore I will work, I will save, I will sacrifice, I will endure, I will fight cheerfully and do my utmost, as if the issue of the whole struggle depended on me alone."
>
> The crisis we are facing today . . . [requires] our best effort, and our willingness to believe in ourselves and to believe in our capacity to perform great deeds; to believe that together, with God's help, we can and will resolve the problems which now confront us.
>
> And, after all, why shouldn't we believe that? We are Americans.

Note: Treptow was killed in the Chateau-Thierry area of France. Official records give July 29, 1918, as the date of his death, although it is possible that he was killed on July 28.

EDDIE RICKENBACKER,
ACE OF ACES

*T*o become a pilot, Eddie Rickenbacker had to fib about his age—the second time he'd had to do so to get a job. The first time came in 1904, when he was thirteen. His father had died, and Rickenbacker quit school to help support his family. Child labor laws required workers to be fourteen, so he claimed that age to get a job in a glass factory for $3.50 a week. But he soon developed an interest in the new "horseless carriages" and turned himself into one of the nation's best race car drivers, competing in the Indianapolis 500 and setting a world speed record of 134 miles per hour at Daytona.

When the United States entered World War I, Rickenbacker enlisted and went to France, hoping to become a pilot. "War flying is for youngsters just out of school," he was told. So now he had to claim he was *younger* than his twenty-seven years. He talked his way into the Army Air Service, took pilot's training, and wound up in the 94th Aero Pursuit Squadron, the famous "Hat-in-the-Ring Squadron." In less than three months, he shot down five enemy planes, becoming the second American ace of the war.

On September 25, 1918, while flying alone near Verdun, Rickenbacker spotted seven German aircraft—two reconnaissance planes escorted by five fighter planes. Climbing as high as he could, he switched off his engine, glided toward the rear fighter, and shot it down. Instead of scrambling to safety, he roared into the enemy formation. "I saw tracer bullets go whizzing and streaking past my face," he later recalled. He managed to shoot down one of the reconnaissance planes before turning for home.

For his courage that day, Rickenbacker was awarded the Medal of Honor. Before the war's end, he shot down twenty-six enemy craft, an American record that earned him the title "Ace of Aces."

SERGEANT YORK

*T*he most famous American warrior of World War I was a reluctant hero. When drafted, he struggled with the idea of fighting. Thirty-year-old Alvin York, a backwoods Tennessee farmer, had only recently given up his "hog wild" days of drinking and carousing and had asked his sweetheart to marry him. He had embraced the pacifist Christian faith of his widowed mother. He later said, "I didn't want to go and kill."

York spent weeks wrestling with his conscience, and finally decided that although he hated war, going was the right thing to do. He left for France convinced that "we were to be peacemakers. . . . We were to help make peace, the only way the Germans would understand."

He had grown up hunting, and the other soldiers soon discovered that he was an astonishing shot. On October 8, 1918, in the Argonne Forest, his marksmanship saved American lives when his patrol ran into a German machine-gun nest. "Our boys just went down like the long grass before the mowing machine at home," he recalled. He went on the attack, picking off twenty-five Germans with his rifle and pistol before their commander surrendered. By the time York and his companions got back to headquarters, they had a long line of prisoners. "Well, York, I hear you have captured the whole German army," an officer said. York replied that he had only 132.

Promoted to sergeant and awarded the Medal of Honor, he was greeted in New York City after the war with a ticker tape parade. But he declined to grow rich off his fame. He returned to Tennessee, married his fiancée, established a school for mountain children, and farmed the land as he had before.

THE AMERICAN LEGION

$\int$ hortly after World War I ended, twenty officers of the American Expeditionary Forces met in Paris with orders to confer on how the Army could improve troop morale. One of the officers, Lt. Col. Theodore Roosevelt Jr., son of President Theodore Roosevelt, suggested an idea that had already crossed many of the men's minds: an organization in which veterans could stay in touch, help each other, and work together after the fighting was over.

The officers wasted no time putting the idea into action. On March 15, 1919, about one thousand US soldiers gathered in Paris for the very first meeting of the American Legion.

Today the Legion is the nation's largest veterans' organization, with nearly two million members. Men and women may join if they have served honorably in the US armed forces during times of hostilities, such as World War II, the Korean War, the Vietnam War, the Persian Gulf War, the Iraq War, and the War in Afghanistan.

The Legion's purpose is partly to help veterans continue friendships formed during military service. It also gives members a way to keep serving their country. The American Legion has built parks and playgrounds, donated equipment to hospitals and fire halls, sponsored Boy Scout troops and youth baseball leagues, promoted the study of the Constitution in schools, and much more.

For God and Country is the American Legion motto. The organization has 12,000 posts worldwide. There is probably one near you, and your community is almost certainly a better place for it.

MARY MCLEOD BETHUNE

*A*s a girl, Mary McLeod Bethune dreamed of becoming a missionary in Africa. Born in 1875 to parents who had been slaves, she grew up near Maysville, South Carolina, working in cotton fields. Her burning desire to learn made her the star student in Maysville's one-room school for black children. Scholarships led to more schooling in North Carolina, and then at Dwight Moody's Institute for Home and Foreign Missions in Chicago. After finishing her studies, she learned there were "no openings for Negro missionaries in Africa."

Undeterred, she embarked on a career as an educator. On October 3, 1904, with $1.50 in cash—all the money she had—she opened the Daytona Literacy and Industrial School for Training Negro Girls in a cottage in Daytona Beach, Florida. The school started with five pupils. Bethune used crates for desks, made ink from elderberries, and sold sweet potato pies to raise funds. She convinced wealthy businessmen to support her efforts. "Invest in a human soul," she urged them. The school grew, and today it lives on as Bethune-Cookman University.

One night in 1920, eighty hooded Ku Klux Klansmen appeared outside the school, waving a burning cross. They had heard Bethune was registering black voters, and threatened to burn the school. "If you do, we'll rebuild it," she answered. The Klansmen rode away, and the next day Bethune led a procession of blacks to the polls.

Her courage won the admiration of Franklin and Eleanor Roosevelt. In 1936, she became the first black woman to head a federal agency, the Division of Negro Affairs of the National Youth Administration. Bethune joined other prominent blacks to form FDR's "black cabinet," an informal committee that advised the president on racial issues.

FEAR ITSELF

Franklin Delano Roosevelt entered politics because he was a man of ambition and because he wanted to serve his country. His plans were almost cut short while vacationing at Campobello Island in New Brunswick, Canada, in 1921 when he came down with what, at first, seemed to be a cold. He lost his appetite, his back began to ache, and his left leg went numb. A few days later, he couldn't stand. At age thirty-nine Roosevelt was diagnosed with polio. Paralyzed from the waist down, he watched as the muscles of his legs began wasting away.

Roosevelt was determined to beat the disease. For months he crawled from room to room in his house and dragged himself hand over hand up the stairs, gritting his teeth but never asking for help. Every day, he strapped steel braces onto his legs and tried hobbling on crutches to the end of his long driveway. Through rigorous exercise he developed tremendous upper body strength. "Maybe my legs aren't so good," he said, "but look at those shoulders." Despite his efforts, he never again walked without aid.

He did, however, make it to the White House, where he led the nation through the Great Depression and World War II. President Roosevelt worked with such vigor that millions of Americans never realized the full extent of his disability. Once someone asked him how he had so much perseverance. He smiled and answered, "If you have to spend two years in bed trying to wiggle your big toe, everything else seems easy."

Roosevelt knew that our trials often make us stronger. "The only thing we have to fear is fear itself," he told Americans during the Depression. The thirty-second US president did his best to live by those words.

THE FATHER OF
MODERN ROCKETRY

*T*he age of rockets began on March 16, 1926, when Robert H. Goddard launched the world's first liquid-fueled rocket at a farm in Auburn, Massachusetts.

Goddard had become fascinated with the idea of space travel as a boy when he read H. G. Wells's science fiction classic *War of the Worlds*. As a student and then a physics professor, he experimented with different rocket designs. His work went virtually unnoticed. In fact, the most publicity he received was when the *New York Times*, hearing of his theory that someday a rocket might reach the moon, printed a jeering editorial declaring that Dr. Goddard "seems to lack the knowledge ladled out daily in high schools."

Goddard kept at his work. For nearly twenty years he tried experiment after experiment. None of the rockets he built would fly. Then came the cold March day in 1926 when he drove to his aunt Effie's farm, set up a ten-foot-tall rocket he had dubbed Nell, and lit the fuse.

For an instant the missile did nothing, then suddenly it screeched off the pad, shot forty-one feet into the air at sixty miles per hour, and thumped down in a cabbage patch 184 feet away. The flight lasted only two and a half seconds, but it was two and a half seconds that ultimately led human beings into outer space.

In the following years Goddard kept developing his rockets, shooting them higher and faster. He continued to work in relative obscurity.

Not until after his death in 1945 did the world realize his achievements. Rockets based on Goddard's work eventually carried men to the moon.

Today Robert Goddard is remembered as the father of modern rocketry. NASA's Goddard Space Flight Center in Greenbelt, Maryland, is named in his honor.

THE SPIRIT OF ST. LOUIS

On the rainy morning of May 20, 1927, twenty-five-year-old Charles Lindbergh climbed into a tiny one-seat plane at Roosevelt Field in Long Island, New York. Minutes later the aircraft was heading down the unpaved runway. Lindbergh was about to try what no one else had been able to do: fly nonstop from New York to Paris.

He had named his plane *Spirit of St. Louis* because several St. Louis businessmen had helped pay for it. To cut down on weight, he was going without a radio or parachute. Yet the plane was so loaded with fuel it barely cleared the telephone wires at the end of the runway as it headed toward the shifting airs of the northern Atlantic.

For the next thirty-three and a half hours, the young pilot bounced through rain squalls and crossed frozen deserts of ice. In the blackness of night, he flew into a cloud that threatened to encrust his wings with ice and drag him into the sea.

As the hours mounted, he battled fatigue. To stay awake, he held his eyelids open with his fingers.

The sun finally rose. A few hours later, Lindbergh saw specks on the water—fishing boats. He had reached the coast of Ireland.

On he flew, over England. Another night fell as he crossed the English Channel to France. "I almost hated to see the lights of Paris," he said, "because the night was clear and I still had gas in my tanks."

Lindbergh's courage and determination thrilled people the world over. Today his *Spirit of St. Louis* hangs in the Smithsonian's Air and Space Museum in Washington, DC. It is still hard to believe he managed to cross the Atlantic alone in such a fragile craft. It may have been the most daring flight ever.

PHILO FARNSWORTH, THE FORGOTTEN INVENTOR

On September 7, 1927, in a San Francisco laboratory, inventor Philo Farnsworth and a small team of assistants placed a slide containing an image of a triangle in front of a machine Farnsworth called an Image Dissector, and then gathered around a receiving tube on the other side of a partition. As they watched, one line of the triangle appeared in a small bluish square of light on the receiver. At Farnsworth's instructions, someone rotated the slide. As if by magic, the image of the line on the receiver turned as well.

"That's it, folks!" Farnsworth exclaimed. "We've done it! There you have electronic television!"

As Farnsworth refined his device, he surely thought that fame and fortune awaited him. It wasn't to be. Russian immigrant Vladimir Zworykin, who had also been trying to develop a television system, claimed that *he* was the true inventor of TV. Zworykin worked for the Radio Corporation of America (RCA), which began to sell television sets and broadcast programs.

Years of legal battles followed, and though the US Patent Office sided with Farnsworth, he lost other lawsuits, and years passed before RCA paid him for his work.

Farnsworth never received much public recognition for his world-changing invention. Ironically, he appeared on national television only once. In 1957, he was a mystery guest on the TV game show *I've Got a*

Secret. A panel of celebrities peppered him with questions about his secret, but failed to guess what it was: "I invented electronic television." His prize for stumping the panel was eighty dollars and a carton of cigarettes.

Nearly two decades after Farnsworth's death, his home state of Utah placed a statue of him in Statuary Hall in the US Capitol. On the statue's base are inscribed the words *Father of Television*.

JESSE OWENS AT BERLIN

esse Owens came from humble beginnings—he was the son of a sharecropper and grandson of a slave. When he was a boy in Cleveland, a coach saw him running in gym class and invited him to join the track team. Jesse couldn't go to the team's after-school practices because he had a job to help support his family, so the coach trained him in the mornings. By the time he was in college, Owens was a star. At one track meet, in a span of forty-five minutes, he broke three world records and tied a fourth.

In 1936 he traveled to Berlin to compete in the Summer Olympics, in which Adolf Hitler planned to show the world the "Aryan superiority" of German youth.

In three days Owens won three gold medals in the 100-meter dash, 200-meter dash, and long jump. A few days later, American athletes Marty Glickman and Sam Stroller—both Jewish—were yanked from the 400-meter relay team to appease Hitler. The American coach told Owens that he and Frank Metcalfe would run in their place. "I've won the races I set out to win," Owens protested. "Let Marty and Sam run." The coach insisted, and on August 9, 1936, Owens won his fourth gold medal.

Hitler, who had stopped shaking each winner's hand, was asked if he wanted to make an exception for Jesse. The Führer shouted: "Do you really think I would allow myself to be photographed shaking hands with a Negro?" But German crowds cheered the American champion with the cry of *"Oh-vens! Oh-vens!"* African American athletes won almost one-quarter of all US medals in the 1936 Olympics, a firm rebuke of Hitler's venomous theories about the so-called superiority of the Aryan race.

DISNEY'S FOLLIES

oday Walt Disney is regarded as one of the geniuses of American popular culture. But throughout his career, he heard people say, "It won't work." As a young man, he tried to get a job with the *Kansas City Star*, but the newspaper said no. He started a little company called Laugh-O-Gram Films to make cartoons, but the money ran out, and he had to declare bankruptcy.

Walt moved to Los Angeles but failed to find a job, so in 1923 he started his own studio in the back of a real estate office. In 1928, when he had an idea for a cartoon rodent, people in Hollywood scoffed. He sold his car to help finance the project. The public fell in love with Mickey Mouse.

A few years later, Walt decided to make a film called *Snow White*. The experts called it "Disney's Folly." Bankers refused to help him. In 1937 it became a huge box office hit.

Several years later, Walt set his heart on building a theme park. Colleagues advised against it. Roy Disney, his brother and business partner, worried that it was too risky. Walt pushed ahead, and in 1955 the world went wild over Disneyland.

"I can't believe that there are any heights that can't be scaled by a man who knows the secrets of making dreams come true," Walt Disney said. "This special secret, it seems to me, can be summarized in four Cs. They are curiosity, confidence, courage, and constancy, and the greatest of all is confidence."

AMELIA EARHART'S
LAST FLIGHT

On July 2, 1937, aviator Amelia Earhart took off from Lae, New Guinea, in her twin-engine Lockheed Electra and flew east into overcast skies toward Howland Island, a sliver of land 2,600 miles away in the Pacific Ocean. She was never seen again.

At the time she disappeared, Earhart was a world-renowned aviation pioneer. In 1932 she had become the first woman to make a solo, non-stop flight across the Atlantic, an accomplishment that earned her the Distinguished Flying Cross. The next year she became the first woman to fly nonstop, coast-to-coast across the United States. As she neared her fortieth birthday, she set her sights on a new goal, the "one flight which I most wanted to attempt," a circumnavigation of the globe near the equator.

When she left New Guinea with her navigator, Fred Noonan, Earhart had completed all but 7,000 miles of her 29,000-mile journey. The Coast Guard cutter *Itasca* waited off Howland Island, where the plane was to refuel. As the arrival time approached, the *Itasca* received the message "We must be on you, but we cannot see you. Fuel is running low. Been unable to reach you by radio. We are flying at 1,000 feet." Efforts to make radio contact failed. A massive search followed but turned up no trace of the plane.

Even today, searches for clues about Earhart's fate continue. Some experts believe her plane ran out of fuel and had to ditch in the Pacific.

Others theorize that Earhart and Noonan reached another island, where they eventually perished. So far, no solid evidence has turned up. Earhart's sense of adventure and determination to fly farther than before still fascinate Americans. "Courage is the price that life exacts for granting peace," she wrote, words she lived by to the end.

ELEANOR ROOSEVELT

*F*or nearly a century and a half, most First Ladies stayed out of the limelight, their public duties limited to greeting White House guests and hosting state dinners. Eleanor Roosevelt changed that during the years her husband, Franklin, was president, from 1933 to 1945. She was the first First Lady to hold press conferences and address a national party convention. She gave scores of speeches, authored magazine articles, wrote a newspaper column, and captured the country's imagination.

Eleanor seemed to be everywhere, visiting coal miners in Appalachia, sharecroppers in cotton fields, and soldiers overseas. Sometimes FDR would say, "About that situation, my Missus told me . . ."

In November 1938 the outspoken First Lady attended a conference in Birmingham, Alabama, where segregation laws required blacks and whites to sit apart at public gatherings. She arrived at the auditorium, took one look at the whites sitting on one side of the aisle and blacks on the other, and took her seat on the black side.

After a few moments a police officer said she would have to move. The chief of police had threatened to arrest anyone who broke the segregation laws. Move she did—by placing her chair in the aisle between both sections, sitting beside whites *and* blacks.

For the rest of the four-day conference, she carried a folding chair from meeting to meeting. In every room she sat in the middle, refusing to be segregated, a symbol of the need for all Americans to come together. "We are the leading democracy of the world," she told the conference, "and as such must prove to the world that democracy is possible and capable of living up to the principles upon which it was founded."

THE IRON HORSE

On May 2, 1939, loudspeakers at Yankee Stadium stunned the crowd with the announcement that New York first baseman Lou Gehrig would not be in the day's lineup. Gehrig, a fan favorite, had a lifetime batting average of .340. He had slugged 493 home runs, including 23 grand slams, and averaged a staggering 147 RBIs per season. But his most amazing stat was his streak of 2,130 consecutive games played. For thirteen years, he had played through good times and bad without missing a game. The son of working-class German immigrants showed up day after day to give his best in his steady, quiet way. His endurance earned him the nickname "the Iron Horse."

But Gehrig had not played well lately. He could tell something was wrong with his body. He had trouble hitting the ball. In the field, he even had trouble getting to first base in time to take a throw. "I'm benching myself," he told his manager. "For the good of the team."

Medical exams brought a bleak diagnosis: amyotrophic lateral sclerosis (ALS), a disease of the nervous system. The chances of long-term survival were slim. Gehrig took the blow with courage and grace, telling friends he was hoping for the best.

On July 4, 1939, Lou Gehrig stood on the field in a packed Yankee Stadium to say good-bye. Surrounded by friends, family, teammates, and fans, the first baseman stepped up to the microphones. "For the past two weeks you have been reading about the bad break I got," he said. "Yet today I consider myself the luckiest man on the face of this earth."

Gehrig died two years later from the disease that now bears his name. Sports fans still remember him as the Iron Horse.

FDR'S "DAY OF INFAMY" ADDRESS

On December 8, 1941, the day after the attack on Pearl Harbor, a somber President Franklin Delano Roosevelt strapped his steel braces onto his legs and walked into the US House chamber, leaning on his son Jimmy's arm. There he addressed a joint session of Congress and asked for a declaration of war against Japan:

> Yesterday, December 7, 1941, a date which will live in infamy, the United States of America was suddenly and deliberately attacked by naval and air forces of the Empire of Japan.
>
> The United States was at peace with that nation and, at the solicitation of Japan, was still in conversation with its government and its emperor looking toward the maintenance of peace in the Pacific. . . . The attack yesterday on the Hawaiian Islands has caused severe damage to American naval and military forces. Very many American lives have been lost. . . . As commander in chief of the Army and Navy I have directed that all measures be taken for our defense.
>
> Always will we remember the character of the onslaught against us.
>
> No matter how long it may take us to overcome this premeditated invasion, the American people, in their righteous might, will win through to absolute victory.
>
> I believe I interpret the will of the Congress and of the people when I assert that we will not only defend ourselves to the uttermost but will

make very certain that this form of treachery shall never endanger us again.

Hostilities exist. There is no blinking at the fact that our people, our territory, and our interests are in grave danger.

With confidence in our armed forces, with the unbounded determination of our people, we will gain the inevitable triumph. So help us God.

BOB HOPE, HONORARY VETERAN

One day comedian Bob Hope got a suggestion from a sponsor: broadcast his popular radio program from March Field, an army air base at Riverside, California. "Why should we drag the whole show down there?" Hope asked. But he consented, and on May 6, 1941, he performed for hundreds of cheering troops.

That one show changed his life. He couldn't get out of his mind the appreciative response of the young recruits. Seven months later, Japan attacked Pearl Harbor. Throughout the rest of World War II, with only two exceptions, Hope aired his shows from US military installations. He went wherever the soldiers were fighting—Europe, North Africa, the Pacific.

"When the time for recognition of service to the nation in wartime comes to be considered, Bob Hope should be high on the list," John Steinbeck wrote in a newspaper column. "He gets laughter wherever he goes from men who need laughter."

After the war Hope became one of America's most popular entertainers. (And one of its most successful immigrants. His family had emigrated from England when he was a boy, coming through Ellis Island.) He never forgot the troops. For more than half a century, through the Cold War, Korean War, Vietnam War, Persian Gulf War, and times of peace, he led tours around the globe to perform for soldiers. "I wouldn't trade it for my entire career," he said. "Until you've actually seen them in action, you have no conception of their courage." Millions watched his televised Christmas shows for the troops.

Hope received all kinds of awards for service to country, including the Congressional Gold Medal and Presidential Medal of Freedom. In 1997, six years before his death, Congress made him an "Honorary Veteran," the first time it had ever bestowed such a tribute. Hope said it was the greatest honor he had ever received.

I SHALL RETURN

*W*aves of Japanese troops assaulted the Philippine Islands at the outset of World War II, steadily overpowering Filipino and American defenders. The US forces commanded by General Douglas MacArthur fought back but were short on supplies and vastly outnumbered. Surrender was inevitable.

MacArthur received personal instructions to proceed to Australia without his soldiers, where he could organize a counterattack. He refused to leave his hungry, desperate men behind until President Roosevelt issued an order he could not ignore. The heartbroken general slipped past the Japanese navy by boat and plane to reach Australia. Once there, on March 20, 1942, he made a solemn pledge to his men back in the Philippines: "I shall return."

In April, unable to hold out any longer, some 75,000 American and Filipino troops on the Bataan Peninsula surrendered to the Japanese—the largest mass surrender in American history. The captors beat and murdered many POWs during the infamous sixty-five-mile Bataan Death March to prison camps. American and Filipino soldiers on nearby Corregidor Island fared no better. The Japanese also imprisoned thousands of American and other Allied civilians living in the Philippines, and for months assumed no responsibility for feeding them.

By the summer of 1942, the United States had launched a counteroffensive. For two and a half years, Allied forces fought their way across the Pacific, island by island. On October 20, 1944, MacArthur finally waded back onto the Philippines' shores to make good on his pledge and liberate the islands.

BUTCH O'HARE SAVES
THE *LEXINGTON*

O n April 21, 1942, a nervous Lt. Cdr. Edward "Butch" O'Hare stood beside his wife, Rita, at the White House while Franklin Delano Roosevelt awarded him the Congressional Medal of Honor for "one of the most daring, if not the most daring single action in the history of combat aviation."

Butch O'Hare never really wanted a medal—just a chance to do his job. On February 20, 1942, he was on board the aircraft carrier *Lexington* in the South Pacific when radar picked up a formation of Japanese bombers closing in fast. The *Lexington* quickly launched fighters to intercept the oncoming planes. By the time O'Hare got aloft in his Grumman F4F-3 Wildcat, there was no chance to "get in on the brawl," as he later put it, because other fighters had done a magnificent job breaking up the attack.

Then came a frantic message from the *Lexington*: a second wave of Japanese bombers had appeared. Only two Wildcats were in position to head them off—Butch and his wingman "Duff" Dufilho. Dufilho soon discovered that his guns wouldn't fire. That left Butch to fight off the bombers, which were minutes away from his carrier.

Roaring at the bombers, O'Hare began picking them off with deadly aim, one at a time. Sailors on deck watched in awe as he shot down five planes and disabled a sixth, all in a matter of minutes. He stopped only when he ran out of ammunition. When he landed, his first words were, "Just load those ammo belts, and I'll get back up." There was no need—his shooting had broken up the attack and saved the *Lexington*.

Twenty-one months later, Butch O'Hare's plane disappeared over the Pacific during a night attack against some Japanese torpedo bombers. In 1949 Chicago renamed its airport O'Hare International Airport in honor of the Navy's first flying ace.

THE NAVAJO CODE TALKERS

*D*uring World War II, the US military faced a deadly communications problem in the Pacific: the Japanese often succeeded in intercepting and deciphering Allied messages. It was getting harder and harder to invent codes the enemy couldn't crack.

The solution came from the Navajo "code talkers," men from the Navajo nation who put their native language to work for the Marines. In May 1942, twenty-nine Navajo recruits gathered in San Diego and soon began devising a code that proved to be one of the most foolproof in the history of warfare. How did the ingenious code work?

The code talkers started by creating strings of seemingly unrelated Navajo words. Once translated into English, the first letter of each word was used to spell out a message. More than one Navajo word could be used to stand for each English letter, making the code even more confusing to the Japanese. For example, for the letter *a*, code talkers could use the word *wol-la-chee* (ant) or *be-la-sana*, (apple). One way to send the word *navy* was *tsah* (needle) *wol-la-chee* (ant) *ah-keh-di-glini* (victor) *tsah-ah-dzoh* (yucca). The code talkers also used Navajo words for military terms. The Navajo word for *hummingbird* stood for a fighter plane.

More than four hundred Navajos served as US Marine code talkers in the Pacific, sending radio messages between command posts and front lines. The Japanese never broke the code. These brave men saved countless lives and helped speed the Allied victory. At the battle of Iwo Jima alone, six code talkers sent and received more than eight hundred messages in the first two days of fighting, all without error. One signal officer later said, "Were it not for the Navajos, the Marines would never have taken Iwo Jima."

ROSIE THE RIVETER

On November 28, 1942, during World War II, the assembly line at Ford Motor Company's huge Willow Run plant at Ypsilanti, Michigan, turned out its first production bomber, a B-24 Liberator. By the time the plant reached its peak, in summer 1944, it was producing a bomber an hour—thanks in no small part to Rosie the Riveter.

With so many men fighting overseas, war factories across the United States faced a critical labor shortage. Posters bearing slogans such as "Do the Job He Left Behind" and "Soldiers Without Guns" appealed for women workers. Millions of American women who had never worked outside the home traded aprons for overalls and went to work in the factories.

Soon they were tackling jobs only men had done before. They learned welding, drafting, and sheet-metal work to build airplanes, Jeeps, and ships. They packed ammo and tested guns, worked in lumber and steel mills, drove trucks, operated cranes, and more.

The women often worked six days a week, giving up vacations and holidays as long as the war dragged on. They put up with noisy, gritty working conditions and then, in the evening, many trudged home to take care of their children. All the while, they reminded themselves that their sacrifices would shorten the war and bring loved ones home.

An admiring public nicknamed the women defense workers "Rosie the Riveter." Their tough resourcefulness helped transform America into the arsenal of democracy.

THE FOUR CHAPLAINS

In the early hours of February 3, 1943, the US Army troopship *Dorchester* steamed through the icy waters of "torpedo alley" some one hundred miles off the coast of Greenland. The ship, carrying more than nine hundred men, was having a rough go of it. Winter winds screeched across the North Atlantic, and heavy seas pounded the bow. Beneath the frenzied surface lurked a German submarine.

At 12:55 a.m. a torpedo ripped into the *Dorchester*'s side, and immediately the ship started to sink. Desperate soldiers rushed topside, stumbling toward lifeboats and jumping overboard. Amid the confusion, four army chaplains worked quietly and methodically, calming the soldiers, directing them toward lifeboats, and handing out life jackets. When they ran out, they took off their own life jackets and put them on other men.

They were four chaplains of different faiths: Jewish rabbi Alexander Goode, Catholic priest John Washington, and Protestant ministers George Fox and Clark Poling. They had joined the US Army to tend to the spiritual needs of the troops. Now, in this hour of urgent need, they put their courage and faith to work so others might live.

As the ship slid beneath the surface, soldiers in the lifeboats took one last look at the *Dorchester*. They saw the four chaplains standing on deck, arms linked, praying.

Rescue ships plucked 230 men from the sea, but 672 died in the freezing Atlantic. The four chaplains were not among the survivors.

"They were always together," one of the soldiers later said. "They carried their faith together." The four chaplains died as they lived, serving their country, their fellow men, and God.

THE TUSKEGEE AIRMEN

*D*uring World War II, the US military had a policy of racial segregation. Blacks trained and fought in separate units from whites. Before 1941 blacks weren't allowed to serve as pilots. Many people said they weren't smart or disciplined enough to fly combat aircraft. But that year, under pressure from black leaders and Congress, the Army Air Corps opened an air base in Tuskegee, Alabama, and began to train black airmen.

The Tuskegee Army Air Base trained not only pilots but navigators, bombardiers, mechanics, and all the other personnel needed to keep planes in the air. Soon the Tuskegee Airmen were proving that they could fly aircraft as well as anyone else. Still, some people asked, "How will they do in combat?"

Beginning in 1943, the army sent 450 Tuskegee pilots to North Africa and Europe to fight in the war. They flew fighters that escorted bombers over enemy territory. The Tuskegee Airmen painted the tails of their fighters red, and as their reputation for protecting planes grew, bomber crews started asking for the "Red Tail Angels" as escorts.

The Tuskegee Airmen flew hundreds of missions and rarely lost a bomber they were assigned to protect from enemy fire. Many became decorated war heroes. About 150 Tuskegee pilots lost their lives in combat or in accidents.

In 1946, after the war was over, training at Tuskegee ended. By then 992 pilots had graduated from the program. They had shown the world they could fly with the best, and their superb record paved the way for ending racial discrimination in the military.

THE JEFFERSON MEMORIAL

*O*ne of the most eloquent tributes to Thomas Jefferson, author of the Declaration of Independence and third president of the United States, came in 1943, during World War II, when Franklin D. Roosevelt dedicated the Jefferson Memorial in Washington, DC:

Today, in the midst of a great war for freedom, we dedicate a shrine to freedom. . . . [Jefferson] faced the fact that men who will not fight for liberty can lose it. We, too, have faced that fact. . . .

He lived in a world in which freedom of conscience and freedom of mind were battles still to be fought through—not principles already accepted of all men. We, too, have lived in such a world. . . .

He loved peace and loved liberty—yet on more than one occasion he was forced to choose between them. We, too, have been compelled to make that choice. . . .

The Declaration of Independence and the very purposes of the American Revolution itself, while seeking freedoms, called for the abandonment of privileges. . . .

Thomas Jefferson believed, as we believe, in Man. He believed, as we believe, that men are capable of their own government, and that no king, no tyrant, no dictator can govern for them as well as they can govern for themselves.

He believed, as we believe, in certain inalienable rights. He, as we, saw those principles and freedoms challenged. He fought for them, as we fight for them. . . .

The words which we have chosen for this Memorial speak Jefferson's noblest and most urgent meaning, and we are proud indeed to understand it and share it:

"I have sworn, upon the altar of God, eternal hostility against every form of tyranny over the mind of man."

O n August 2, 1943, torpedo boat PT-109 was patrolling the Blackett Strait in the Solomon Islands when a shape loomed in the darkness off the starboard bow. A crewman yelled, "Ship at two o'clock!" but it was too late. The Japanese destroyer *Amagiri* plowed into the little boat, slicing it in half. The collision threw the PT's commander, Lt. John F. Kennedy Jr., hard against the side of the cockpit, and as gasoline ignited on the water around him, he thought, *So this is how it feels to die.*

Two crew members were killed in the crash. The eleven who survived, including Kennedy, clung to wreckage. When the remains of the hull began to sink, they made a four-hour swim to a deserted island three miles away. Most of the crew clung to a large piece of timber as they swam, but one man was badly burned, so Kennedy clenched the straps of the man's life jacket in his teeth and towed him, swimming the breaststroke.

Leaving his crew on the island, Kennedy swam out again, hoping to flag down another PT boat, but none appeared. Exhausted, he barely made it back to the island. The next day he led his men to another islet. Several times he ventured out into the shark-infested waters, looking for help, but found none.

On August 6, two Solomon Islanders in a dugout canoe found the stranded sailors. Kennedy carved a message onto a coconut, which they took to Allied troops: NAURO ISL NATIVE KNOWS POSIT HE CAN PILOT 11 ALIVE NEED SMALL BOAT KENNEDY. Within two days, the PT crew was rescued. When he became president of the United States, Kennedy kept the coconut with its scratched message on his desk in the Oval Office to remind himself of the awful ordeal and his two lost comrades.

IF ANY BLAME

*I*n early June 1944, southern England swarmed with Allied troops preparing for one of the greatest events of World War II—a massive invasion of northern France. The Allies had spent months getting ready for D-Day. The plan: about 2,700 ships carrying landing craft and 176,000 men would cross the English Channel and assault German fortifications across a sixty-mile front in Normandy.

General Dwight D. Eisenhower, commander of the invasion, originally chose June 5 as D-Day, but bad weather and rough seas forced a delay. Then Eisenhower received a new weather forecast. The skies would clear and the seas would calm just long enough to launch the invasion the next day. But the window of opportunity would be short.

The general gave the order: "Okay, let's go." Then he went to his portable desk, scribbled the following note, and slipped it into his wallet to use in case things went badly.

> Our landings in the Cherbourg-Havre area have failed to gain a satisfactory foothold and I have withdrawn the troops. My decision to attack at this time and place was based on the best information available. The troops, the air and the Navy did all that bravery and devotion to duty could do. If any blame or fault attaches to the attempt it is mine alone.

It was a statement Eisenhower never had to use. His words, however, remind us that democracies need leaders who have the courage to make the tough calls and then take the heat for them, when necessary.

THE PIED PIPER OF SAIPAN

On his first night on the island of Saipan in June 1944, Marine private Guy Gabaldon slipped out of camp on his own and returned with two Japanese prisoners. His commanders told him that if he left his post again, he'd be court-martialed. But the next night he disappeared again and came back with fifty prisoners. After that, his superiors let him go on his "lone-wolf" missions whenever he wanted.

Gabaldon wasn't simply after prisoners. He was trying to save lives. American troops had stormed Saipan to break the Japanese defense line in the Pacific and secure a site for an air base. The Japanese tried to hold the island with desperate suicide charges. Gabaldon figured that more prisoners meant fewer casualties.

Just eighteen years old, Guy Gabaldon had learned street smarts from growing up in East Los Angeles barrios. He also knew some Japanese, thanks to a childhood friendship with a Japanese-American family. Working alone, he would creep up to an enemy-held cave or bunker, call out that the Marines were nearby, and assure the Japanese that they would be treated with dignity if they would lay down their arms: "I must have seen too many John Wayne movies, because what I was doing was suicidal." But his plan kept working.

One day Gabaldon persuaded some eight hundred Japanese soldiers to surrender and follow him back to the American lines. His astounded comrades nicknamed him the "Pied Piper of Saipan." He captured perhaps 1,500 prisoners. Gabaldon's bravery earned him the Navy Cross, and Hollywood made a movie, *Hell to Eternity*, about him. But his greatest reward was knowing that he had single-handedly saved many American lives.

THE YOUNGEST PILOT
IN THE NAVY

*O*n September 2, 1944, George Herbert Walker Bush, the youngest pilot then serving in the US Navy, climbed into a TBM Avenger torpedo bomber, catapulted off the deck of the carrier *San Jacinto*, and headed toward Chichi Jima, a Japanese island six hundred miles south of Tokyo. With him rode two crewmen, radioman Jack Delaney and gunnery officer Ted White. Their target: a Japanese radio installation.

As Bush dove toward the station, black splotches of antiaircraft fire exploded around the Avenger. "Suddenly there was a jolt, as if a massive fist had crunched into the belly of the plane," he later wrote. "Smoke poured into the cockpit, and I could see flames rippling across the crease of the wing, edging toward the fuel tanks." He managed to unload his bombs on the target and head the Avenger to sea, yelling for his crewmates to bail out. As the aircraft lost altitude, Bush jumped as well, colliding with the plane's tail on the way. He landed bleeding but alive in the water. Delaney and White did not survive—one's parachute failed to open, and the other never made it out of the plane.

Bush climbed into a life raft as Japanese boats sped toward him. US fighter planes drove them back, but currents pushed the raft toward Chichi Jima, where (unbeknownst to Bush) the Japanese had executed and cannibalized American POWs. Using his hands, Bush paddled furiously against the tide.

A few hours later, he saw a periscope break the water's surface, followed by the hull of the sub USS *Finback*. Within minutes, the downed pilot was safely aboard.

The navy sent Bush to Hawaii for rest and recovery. But he couldn't sit still while the war raged, especially when he thought of his lost comrades. So the future president cut short his leave and headed back to the *San Jacinto* to finish his tour of duty.

AUDIE MURPHY

The marines turned him down. They said he was too small. The army paratroopers said no too. But Audie Murphy was used to setbacks. The son of Texas sharecroppers, he helped raise his ten siblings after their father deserted them and their mother died. When the US entered World War II, he was determined to fight. The army finally accepted him in the infantry a few days after his eighteenth birthday.

He fought in the invasion of Sicily, and then in Italy at Salerno, at Anzio, and in the mountains as the Allies pushed to Rome. On January 26, 1945, in eastern France, 250 Germans and six tanks attacked his unit. Ordering his outnumbered men to fall back, Murphy climbed onto a burning tank destroyer and used its machine gun to hold off the enemy. Then, though wounded, he organized a counterattack. For his courage the military awarded him the Medal of Honor.

Before he turned twenty-one, Murphy had become the most decorated American combat soldier of World War II, earning twenty-four medals from the US government, three from France, and one from Belgium.

After the war, Murphy became an actor, making more than forty movies. He starred in *To Hell and Back*, based on his autobiography, and in *The Red Badge of Courage*.

"The true meaning of America, you ask?" Murphy once said. "It's in a Texas rodeo, in a policeman's badge, in the sound of laughing children, in a political rally, in a newspaper. . . . In all these things, and many more, you'll find America. In all these things, you'll find freedom. And freedom is what America means to the world."

THE BUCK STOPS HERE

O n July 17, 1945, the final "Big Three" World War II conference between the United States, Great Britain, and the Soviet Union opened in Potsdam, Germany. There, Harry S. Truman met Winston Churchill and Joseph Stalin for the first time.

Truman entered the conference knowing they had giant issues to resolve: the political future of Eastern Europe, the fate of recently defeated Germany, the still ongoing conflict with Japan. And then there was a question he alone must decide—whether to use the atomic bomb. At Potsdam, Truman received a secret telegram informing him that scientists had set off the world's first nuclear explosion in the New Mexico desert. "Operated on this morning," the telegram said. "Diagnosis not yet complete but results seem satisfactory and already exceed expectation."

When he became president, many political observers held low expectations for Truman, the unassuming son of a Missouri livestock dealer. He quickly proved he was willing to make hard choices and stick by them, a characteristic summed up by a small sign he kept on his desk that read, "The Buck Stops Here."

The saying comes from the slang expression "pass the buck," which means passing responsibility to someone else. "Pass the buck" is said to have come from the game of poker. In frontier days, a knife with a buckhorn handle (made from the antler of a male deer) was often placed on the table to designate the dealer. Players could pass the buck, as the marker was called, to the next player if they did not want to deal the cards.

"The President—whoever he is—has to decide," Truman once said. "He can't pass the buck to anybody. No one else can do the deciding for him. That's his job."

THE AIR FORCE
BIRTHDAY AND FLAG

*T*he United States Air Force was established on September 18, 1947, when the National Security Act, which made the Air Force an independent branch of the military, went into effect. Fittingly, President Harry Truman signed the law aboard the *Sacred Cow*, the C-54 transport plane used for presidential flights in those days.

The beginnings of an American air-going force stretch back to 1907, less than four years after the Wright Brothers' first powered flight, when the US Army Signal Corps formed an Aeronautical Division. In 1909 the Army bought its first plane, the Wright Military Flyer. When World War I started in Europe, the Army owned only five planes. By the end of the war, military strategists realized that to win battles, they must control the skies. During World War II, the US Army Air Forces reached a peak strength of 80,000 planes. The critical role of air power led Truman to make the Air Force a full partner with the Army and Navy.

The US Air Force flag is blue and bears the Air Force coat of arms. The shield carries an image of a pair of wings, a vertical thunderbolt, and lightning flashes—all symbolizing the power to strike from the air. Above the shield, a bald eagle perches in front of a cloud. Thirteen stars surround the coat of arms, representing the thirteen original states. The top three stars also symbolize the Departments of the Army, Navy, and Air Force.

CHUCK YEAGER

ntil October 14, 1947, no one knew if a plane could fly faster than the speed of sound. Aircraft approaching Mach 1 shook violently, as if hitting an invisible wall. Only a year earlier, British pilot Geoffrey De Havilland had died when his plane broke apart flying close to the speed of sound. Scientists theorized that as a plane reached high speeds, sound waves piled up around it, creating a "sound barrier" that held it back.

After World War II the US military and Bell Aircraft developed the X-1, a "bullet with wings" designed to punch a hole through the sound barrier. The test pilot for the rocket-powered plane was twenty-four-year-old Captain Chuck Yeager. A decorated combat ace, Yeager had cheated death more than once. During the war, he'd been shot down over France but eluded the Nazis with the help of the French Resistance, made it back to his squadron, and returned to the skies.

By mid-October 1947 Yeager had flown the X-1 several times over the Mojave Desert, edging closer to the sound barrier. On October 14 he climbed into the plane with two cracked ribs from a fall off a horse—an injury he kept secret so he wouldn't be grounded. A giant B-29 carried the X-1 to 20,000 feet and released it. The plane stalled and dropped 500 feet while Yeager struggled to bring it under control. He fired his rocket engines, climbed to 42,000 feet, leveled off, and fired a rocket again.

Then it happened. The shaking suddenly stopped. "I was so high and so remote, and the airplane was so very quiet that I might have been motionless," Yeager later recalled. But the needle on the speed gauge jumped off the scale. On the ground below, engineers heard the thunder of a sonic boom. Chuck Yeager had punched through the sound barrier.

GIVE 'EM HELL, HARRY

*H*ardly anyone gave President Harry Truman a prayer of a chance to win his 1948 reelection bid against Thomas Dewey of New York. All the pollsters predicted a win for Republican Dewey. Professional gamblers gave odds of fifteen to one against Democrat Truman. Reporters were writing stories about the upcoming Dewey administration.

Truman was about the only one who believed he could win. In September 1948 he left Washington, DC, aboard a railroad car named the *Ferdinand Magellan* for a whistle-stop campaign across America. In speech after speech, town after town, he told people why they should reelect him while the crowds shouted back, "Give 'em hell, Harry!" The *Ferdinand Magellan* traveled nearly 22,000 miles in all. As historian David McCullough points out, never before had a president gone so far to take his case to the people.

Three weeks before the election, *Newsweek* magazine published a survey of fifty political writers. Every single one thought Truman would lose.

On election night, November 2, 1948, Truman went to bed at nine o'clock. He woke up around midnight, turned on the radio, and heard a commentator assure the nation that Dewey would win. Truman clicked him off and went back to sleep.

About four o'clock the next morning, an aide woke the president to tell him that he was ahead by two million votes. "We've got 'em beat," Truman said.

The voters had gone to the polls, elected the man who refused to quit, and reminded the experts that in this magical place called America, it's still the people who get to choose.

ELVIS HITS THE AIRWAVES

On the night Of July 7, 1954, Memphis disc jockey Dewey Phillips played a brand-new recording of the song "That's All Right" sung by nineteen-year-old Elvis Presley, who lived there in Memphis. Right away, listeners starting calling, demanding that he play it again, asking exactly what kind of music it was—blues? rock 'n' roll?—and wanting to know more about the singer.

Dewey played the song fourteen times that night. During one break, he called the Presley home, wanting to get Elvis down to the studio for an interview. Elvis, who'd been told that his record might be on the radio, had been too nervous to listen. "I thought people would laugh at me," he later explained. So he'd gone to the movies.

Dewey asked Elvis's mother to find him, saying, "I played that record of his, and them bird-brain phones haven't stopped ringing since." Mr. and Mrs. Presley hurried to the theater, searched the dark rows, found their son, and hustled the boy off to WHBQ for the interview.

As a child, Elvis Presley soaked up gospel music at church. He listened to country music on *The Grand Ole Opry* radio show, blues singers on the streets of Memphis, and spirituals at tent revivals.

"What kind of singer are you?" the manager of a Memphis recording studio asked him when he made his very first record. "Aw, I sing all kinds," he answered. "Who do you sound like?" she pressed. "I don't sound like nobody," he insisted.

His answer was more than youthful boasting. Presley's unabashedly original style embraced all kinds of American music and crossed all borders of race, class, and region. As biographers have noted, that democratic principle of his music helped win legions of fans.

BORN IN THE USA

On July 9, 1955, "Rock Around the Clock," recorded by Bill Haley & His Comets, hit #1 on the *Billboard* music charts, a spot it would hold for eight weeks. Written by Max Freedman and James E. Myers (a.k.a. Jimmy DeKnight), the song was the first rock 'n' roll recording to top the charts. It had attracted little attention when Haley's band first released it in 1954, but after it appeared in the soundtrack of the movie *The Blackboard Jungle*, millions of young people adopted it as their anthem. "Rock Around the Clock" became a worldwide hit, an event that helped launch the rock 'n' roll revolution.

American music has become the most popular in the world, perhaps because, like America, it reflects traditions and cultures from all over the world. Here are a few styles that have won hearts in every corner of the globe:

BLUES emerged in the South after the Civil War, growing out of African American field songs, ballads, and spirituals.

COUNTRY MUSIC developed in the South in the 1800s, blending British and Irish folk music, blues, Southern religious music, and popular American songs.

JAZZ originated in New Orleans around 1900, spreading to Chicago, Kansas City, Memphis, and cities across the country. Its many roots include African American field songs, hymns, blues, New Orleans brass band music, and European harmonies.

BROADWAY MUSICALS developed in the years following World
War I, evolving out of vaudeville, burlesque, and minstrel
shows. Early musicals blended popular entertainment with
elements of European musical stage traditions.

ROCK 'N' ROLL emerged in the United States in the 1950s,
mixing elements of rhythm and blues, country, dance-band
jazz, and pop music.

REMEMBERING MARTIN LUTHER KING JR.

The Reverend Martin Luther King Jr., born January 15, 1929, was one of the most gifted leaders the country has known. Never was that more evident than on a cold winter night in 1956 in Montgomery, Alabama. King had left his wife and baby at home to attend a meeting at a nearby church. As the meeting wound down, someone rushed in with terrible news: "Your house has been bombed."

King raced home and saw that the bomb had exploded on his front porch. By now the house was full of people. He pushed his way inside and found his family safe.

Outside, however, trouble was stirring. An angry crowd was gathering and wanted revenge against whoever had done this. Several people carried guns and broken bottles. They hurled insults at arriving policemen. The situation was about to spin out of control. That's when King stepped onto his porch.

Silence fell over the crowd.

King told them in a calm voice that his family was all right. "I want you to go home and put down your weapons," he said. He told them violence would not solve their problems; it would only harm their cause. He reminded them of the teachings of the Bible: "We must meet hate with love."

Then something remarkable happened. "Amen," someone said. "God bless you," others called. The crowd, which a moment ago had been on the verge of violence, began to drift apart. A night that had been heading toward chaos came to a quiet, if uneasy, close.

Dr. King spent his life meeting adversity with courage and love and reminding his fellow Americans that "we must forever conduct our struggle on the high plane of dignity and discipline." Good words to remember.

THE FREEDOM RIDERS

On May 4, 1961, thirteen men and women, black and white, boarded a bus in Washington, DC, and set out toward New Orleans. Their mission: challenge segregation practices on public transportation. History remembers them as the Freedom Riders.

The US Supreme Court had already ruled that segregation in interstate bus travel was unconstitutional. But in several Southern states where Jim Crow laws still prevailed, it was considered a crime for whites and blacks to sit side by side on a bus. Yet that's exactly what the Freedom Riders did as they headed south. When they stopped at bus stations, they sat together in segregated waiting rooms and at lunch counters.

By the time they reached the Deep South, trouble was waiting. Near Anniston, Alabama, angry whites firebombed the bus. The Freedom Riders barely escaped with their lives. In Birmingham, riders on a second bus were beaten with clubs and lead pipes. In Montgomery a mob surrounded the church where they sought refuge.

Some civil rights activists urged the Freedom Riders to halt their journey. Despite the danger, *more* people joined the effort. But the Freedom Ride came to an end in Jackson, Mississippi, where police herded more than three hundred to jail.

The Freedom Riders never made it to New Orleans, but they achieved their objective. Inspired by those brave few, more Americans worked to break segregation and lead the country down a better road. In 2001, when some of the Freedom Riders made a fortieth anniversary bus trip retracing their route, the mayor of Anniston welcomed them with the keys to the city.

GODSPEED, JOHN GLENN

$\mathcal{T}$hose words sent Marine lieutenant colonel John H. Glenn on his way as his Atlas rocket lifted off from Cape Canaveral and roared into the sky on February 20, 1962. They came from fellow *Mercury* astronaut Scott Carpenter, on the ground. Tom O'Malley, General Dynamics Corporation project director, added his prayer: "May the good Lord ride with you all the way."

The young test pilot could hear none of this encouragement over the sound of his engines as *Friendship* 7 thundered into space on the US's first attempt to send a man into orbit. The mission went well until, after watching his first sunset in space, Glenn realized that the automatic control system was failing, causing the spacecraft to drift. He calmly switched to a manual system and took command of the capsule, guiding it along at about 17,500 miles per hour.

During the second orbit, a flight controller on the ground noticed a heart-stopping signal: a sensor monitoring the spacecraft's landing system indicated that its heat shield might have come loose. Without it, the capsule would burn to a cinder when it reentered the earth's atmosphere. The ground team decided that the craft's retrorockets, which were designed to be jettisoned before reentry, would be left on to help keep the heat shield in place.

The temperature outside *Friendship* 7 rose to 9,500 degrees Fahrenheit as it slammed into the atmosphere. The capsule entered the communications blackout zone—a brief period when the heat made radio contact impossible. The world held its breath while the spacecraft plummeted.

Would the shield hold? Finally, after what seemed an eternity, Glenn's steady voice crackled through the static: "My condition is good, but that was a real fireball, boy!"

John Glenn had spent five hours in space and circled the earth three times. Americans were headed toward a new frontier.

NO SHORTAGE OF HEROES

On February 28, 1969, Airman First Class John Levitow was lying in a hospital bed, his body covered with forty shrapnel wounds, trying to piece together exactly how he had ended up there. Meanwhile, seven Air Force buddies in South Vietnam were telling themselves they wouldn't be alive if not for Levitow's courage.

Four days earlier, the eight men had flown a night combat mission over South Vietnam aboard an AC-47 gunship, dropping magnesium flares to illuminate enemy positions on the ground. Each flare had a safety pin. Twenty seconds after the pin was pulled and the flare was tossed out a cargo door, it would ignite to 4,000 degrees Fahrenheit, lighting up the countryside.

In the fifth hour of the mission, a Vietcong mortar hit the plane, blasting a hole through a wing and nearly wrenching the gunship out of the sky. Levitow, wounded in the back and legs, had just dragged a bleeding crewmate away from the open cargo door when he saw a smoking flare roll across the floor amid ammunition canisters.

Levitow tried to grab the flare, but it skidded away. In desperation, he threw himself on top. Hugging it to his chest, he dragged himself to the plane's rear, leaving a trail of blood, and hurled the flare through the door. An instant later it burst into a white-hot blaze, but free of the aircraft.

Levitow recovered and went on to fly twenty more combat missions. In 1970 he received the Medal of Honor, an award he accepted with humility. "There are many people who have served, who have done things that have been simply amazing and never been recognized," he said—a good reminder that the US military has no shortage of heroes.

THE POW/MIA FLAG

$\mathcal{T}$ he somber POW/MIA flag, which shows the silhouette of an American prisoner of war in front of a guard tower and barbed wire with the words "You Are Not Forgotten" below, reminds us of the debt we owe the thousands of Americans who have been prisoners of war (POWs), as well as those who have gone missing in action (MIA). The POW/MIA flag is the only flag displayed in the US Capitol Rotunda, where it stands as an emblem of resolve that this nation will never forget those who have suffered in enemy captivity and those missing and unaccounted for.

The Vietnam Veterans Memorial in Washington, DC, is another place where you will see the POW/MIA flag displayed. Inscribed on the monument's wall are more than 58,000 names of soldiers lost during the Vietnam War. Approximately 1,200 of those names represent POWs and MIAs.

Congress has specified six days when it is particularly appropriate to fly the POW/MIA flag: Armed Forces Day, Memorial Day, Flag Day, Independence Day, National POW/MIA Recognition Day (third Friday in September), and Veterans Day.

ONE OF HOLLYWOOD'S FINEST

*J*ohn Ford passionately loves freedom," President Nixon said on March 31, 1973. "John Ford, in his works, has depicted freedom in all of its profound depths. . . . John Ford has fought for freedom, and for that reason it is appropriate that tonight, on behalf of all of the American people, he receives the Medal of Freedom."

The son of Irish immigrants (his real name was John Martin Feeney), director John Ford gave generations of moviegoers his vision of America in dozens of beloved Hollywood films—movies such as *Young Mr. Lincoln* (1939), *The Grapes of Wrath* (1940), *The Searchers* (1956), and *The Man Who Shot Liberty Valance* (1962). But some of his work took place far from American shores.

Though already a famous director, Ford joined the navy during World War II and put together a unit of film crews to document much of the war. In June 1942 he filmed the Battle of Midway from atop the island's powerhouse, a primary target for Japanese bombers. At one point a piece of flying concrete hit him on the head and knocked him out. He came to, grabbed his camera, and kept shooting. When shrapnel tore a hole in his arm, he kept relaying information about the battle's progress to officers on the ground.

Ford went in harm's way from the Pacific to North Africa to the Normandy coast. On D-Day, he oversaw cameramen filming the Allied invasion. After the war, while he continued his legendary Hollywood career, he held the rank of rear admiral in the US Naval Reserve.

Perhaps in part because he knew the cost of freedom, Ford spent a lifetime interpreting his nation's heritage. He accepted the Presidential Medal of Freedom, one of the country's highest civilian honors, with the words, "God bless America."

KEEP SWINGING

$\mathcal{M}$y motto was always to keep swinging. Whether I was in a slump or feeling badly or having trouble off the field, the only thing to do was keep swinging."

That was Henry Aaron's approach to baseball and life, especially in the early 1970s, when "Hammerin' Hank" was playing for the Atlanta Braves and getting close to overtaking Babe Ruth as the all-time home-run leader. As he grew closer to the record-breaking 715 mark, the hate mail began to arrive, and what should have been the best time of his life turned into an ordeal.

Some people couldn't stand the thought of a black man taking Ruth's place as the home-run king. There were thousands of malicious letters. "You will be the most hated man in this country." "You're black so you have no business being here." Even death threats. "I'D LIKE TO KILL YOU!! BANG BANG YOUR DEAD. P.S. It mite happen."

He just kept swinging through the ugliness, quietly carrying on the work of Jackie Robinson, who had first broken baseball's color barrier, and taking comfort from the flood of fan mail urging him on.

On April 8, 1974, Henry Aaron stepped up to the plate in Atlanta and hammered number 715 over the left centerfield wall. As he rounded the bases, millions of Americans cheered. Few realized the full extent of the gauntlet he'd run. But his dignity and perseverance were evident. President Nixon may have said it best: "When I think of Hank Aaron, I think of power and poise, of courage and consistency. But most of all, I think of a true gentleman, an outstanding citizen. On the field and off, Hank Aaron represents America at its very best."

PRESIDENTIAL TRIVIA

*W*hich president was born with the name Leslie Lynch King Jr.? Hint: He was born July 14, 1913, in Omaha, Nebraska. Still don't know? You'll find the answer below.

Who was the first president to be born a US citizen?
Martin Van Buren, December 5, 1782

Who was the only president to have a child born in the White House?
Grover Cleveland, September 9, 1893

Who was the first president born in a log cabin?
Andrew Jackson, March 15, 1767

Who was the last president born in a log cabin?
James Garfield, November 19, 1831

Who was the first president born in a hospital?
Jimmy Carter, October 1, 1924

Who was the only president to undergo a complete name change?
Gerald Ford, born as Leslie Lynch King Jr. His mother's second husband, Gerald R. Ford, later adopted and renamed him.

Who was the only former president to become a member of the US House of Representatives?
John Quincy Adams, 1831

Who was the only former president to become a US senator?
Andrew Johnson, 1875

Who was the only former president to become chief justice of the US Supreme Court?
William Howard Taft, 1921

Which former president joined the Confederate government?
John Tyler, 1861

Who was the first president to reside in Washington, DC?
John Adams, 1800

Who was the first president to visit the West Coast while in office?
Rutherford B. Hayes, 1880

Who was the first president to visit a foreign country while in office?
Theodore Roosevelt, Panama, 1906

THE BIBLE AND THE OATH

*M*any presidents swear the oath of office with a Bible opened to scripture they choose. Here are some examples of Scripture passages used by various presidents.

Theodore Roosevelt, 1905: "But be doers of the word, and not hearers only, deceiving yourselves. For if anyone is a hearer of the word and not a doer, he is like a man who looks intently at his natural face in a mirror." James 1:22–23

Woodrow Wilson, 1917: "God is our refuge and strength, a very present help in trouble." Psalm 46

Franklin D. Roosevelt, 1933, 1937, 1941, 1945: "If I speak in the tongues of men and of angels, but have not love, I am a noisy gong or a clanging cymbal." 1 Corinthians 13

Gerald Ford, 1974: "Trust in the Lord with all your heart, and do not lean on your own understanding. In all your ways acknowledge him, and he will make straight your paths." Proverbs 3:5–6

Jimmy Carter, 1977: "He has told you, O man, what is good; and what does the Lord require of you but to do justice, and to love kindness, and to walk humbly with your God?" Micah 6:8

Ronald Reagan, 1981, 1985: "If my people who are called by my name humble themselves, and pray and seek my face and turn from their wicked ways, then I will hear from heaven, and will forgive their sin and heal their land." 2 Chronicles 7:14

FORGOT TO DUCK

*O*n March 30, 1981, President Ronald Reagan became the only president to survive being shot while in office, and in the process taught the nation something about meeting a crisis with grit, grace, and humor.

It happened sixty-nine days into Reagan's presidency, while leaving a speaking engagement in Washington, DC. As the president walked toward his waiting limousine, a deranged young man fired six shots, grievously wounding White House press secretary Jim Brady and hitting a police officer and Secret Service agent. Another agent shoved Reagan into the limo, and the car sped away.

At first no one realized the president had been shot. Reagan, who felt an excruciating pain, thought he'd broken a rib. He soon began coughing up blood, and the limo headed for the hospital. As he walked into the emergency room, his knees turned rubbery, and he went down.

It would be years before Americans learned how close Reagan came to dying. The assassin's bullet had ricocheted off the limo, pierced his side, and lodged close to his heart. But that night a relieved country laughed as it learned Reagan's first words to First Lady Nancy: "Honey, I forgot to duck" (a line borrowed from boxing great Jack Dempsey a half century earlier when he lost the heavyweight championship).

Reagan's sense of humor never lagged. "I hope you're a Republican," he cracked to a doctor as they wheeled him into the operating room.

The seventy-year-old president returned to the White House a few days later, temporarily weakened but resolved to rededicate himself to his country. A few words in his diary speak volumes of his determination and faith. "Whatever happens now, I owe my life to God and will try to serve him in every way I can," he wrote.

RONALD REAGAN

onald Wilson Reagan, born February 6, 1911, in Tampico, Illinois, became the nation's fortieth president at a time when many said that America's best days were behind us, that the future would be one of fewer opportunities. He spent much of his presidency (1981–89) reminding Americans, again and again, that this country is still a land of boundless potential, a beacon of freedom and hope for the world.

History is a ribbon, always unfurling. History is a journey. And as we continue our journey, we think of those who traveled before us . . . and we see and hear again the echoes of our past: a general falls to his knees in the hard snow of Valley Forge; a lonely president paces the darkened halls and ponders his struggle to preserve the Union; the men of the Alamo call out encouragement to each other; a settler pushes west and sings a song, and the song echoes out forever and fills the unknowing air. It is the American sound. It is hopeful, big-hearted, idealistic, daring, decent, and fair. That's our heritage, that's our song. We sing it still. For all our problems, our differences, we are together as of old. We raise our voices to the God who is the author of this most tender music. And may He continue to hold us close as we fill the world with our sound—in unity, affection, and love—one people under God, dedicated to the dream of freedom that He has placed in the human heart, called upon now to pass that dream on to a waiting and hopeful world.

—RONALD REAGAN, SECOND INAUGURAL ADDRESS

HONORARY CITIZENS OF
THE UNITED STATES

*O*n October 1, 1996, Congress declared Agnes Gonxha Bojaxhiu, better known as Mother Teresa, an honorary citizen of the United States. A native of what is now the Republic of Macedonia, the Roman Catholic nun spent a lifetime helping orphaned and abandoned children, the poor, the sick, and the dying in regions throughout the world, including the United States.

Only a handful of non-citizens have been declared honorary US citizens. According to Congress, it is "an extraordinary honor not lightly conferred nor frequently granted." The other honorary citizens are:

- Winston Churchill (1963), the great British statesmen whose "bravery, charity and valor, both in war and in peace, have been a flame of inspiration in freedom's darkest hour," as President Kennedy put it.
- Raoul Wallenberg (1981), the Swedish businessman who risked his life to save tens of thousands of Hungarian Jews from the Nazis, and who died after being imprisoned by Soviet authorities.
- William Penn (1984), the English Quaker who in 1681 founded Pennsylvania to carry out an experiment based upon representative government, and his wife, Hannah Penn, who administered the Province of Pennsylvania for six years.
- The Marquis de Lafayette (2002), the French soldier and statesman

who fought alongside American Patriots during the Revolutionary War. An American flag flies over his grave in Paris.

- Casimir Pulaski (2009), the Polish soldier and nobleman who fought in the Revolutionary War and became known as "the father of the American cavalry." He died of wounds at the siege of Savannah in Georgia.
- Bernardo de Gálvez (2014), Spanish governor of Louisiana who gave the American patriots invaluable aid during the Revolutionary War.

One day, as Marine corporal Jason Dunham and his buddies swapped talk in their barracks in Iraq, the conversation turned to the best way to survive a hand grenade attack. The corporal suggested covering a grenade with a Kevlar helmet. "I'll bet a Kevlar would stop it," he said.

Dunham, raised in the small town of Scio, New York, was a twenty-two-year-old with a natural gift for leadership. He'd been a star athlete, setting a Scio Central School baseball record for highest batting average. Now a rifle squad leader, he'd extended his enlistment to stay with his comrades in Iraq.

On April 14, 2004, Dunham was on his way to help a Marine convoy that had been ambushed in western Iraq when an insurgent leaped from a car and attacked him. As two Marines rushed to help wrestle the man to the ground, they heard Dunham yell, "No, no, no—watch his hand!" Before they realized what was happening, Dunham threw his helmet and his own body over a live enemy grenade.

The sacrifice helped contain the blast but left Dunham mortally wounded. He died eight days later at the National Naval Medical Center in Bethesda, Maryland.

In January 2007 President George W. Bush awarded the Medal of Honor posthumously to Jason Dunham. "Corporal Dunham saved the lives of two of his men, and showed the world what it means to be a Marine," the president said. He was the first Marine to earn the Medal of Honor for service in Iraq.

Journalist Michael Phillips, author of *The Gift of Valor*, wrote that shortly before leaving for the Persian Gulf, Dunham told friends of his plans to extend his enlistment.

"You're crazy for extending," a fellow Marine had said. "Why?"

"I want to make sure everyone makes it home alive," Jason Dunham answered.

PAT TILLMAN'S SACRIFICE

*A*s an Arizona State University linebacker, Pat Tillman weighed barely two hundred pounds, but he gained a reputation for bone-rattling hits and helped lead his team to the Rose Bowl in 1997. His teammates nicknamed him Braveheart.

After college he turned pro, even though critics said he was too small and slow for the NFL. The Arizona Cardinals took him as their next-to-last draft pick. In 2000 he set a team record with 224 tackles in a single season.

Then came the terrorist attacks of September 11, 2001, and Tillman started thinking about things larger than football. He spoke of family members who had fought for their country, such as his great-grandfather at Pearl Harbor. "I haven't done a damn thing as far as laying myself on the line like that," he said. Eight months later, Tillman shocked the sports world by turning down a $3.6 million football contract and joining the army with his brother.

He enlisted without fanfare, refusing to talk to the press about his decision. "He truly felt committed and felt a sense of honor and duty," his Cardinals coach said. He joined the Army Rangers, an elite outfit that routinely goes in harm's way. On April 22, 2004, he was on patrol near an isolated mud-brick village in southeast Afghanistan, a region rife with terrorist operatives, when gunfire erupted. Pat Tillman was killed by friendly fire. He was twenty-seven.

Controversy later erupted with revelations that army officers initially hid the fact that US troops accidentally shot Tillman. That does not diminish his own sacrifice.

Very few walk away from riches and fame to serve as Tillman did. But there are many who quietly and humbly protect American ideals with everything they have to offer—including their lives. As one of his coaches said, "The spirit of Pat Tillman is the heart of this country."

BE INSPIRED BY HISTORICAL HEROES AND HISTORICAL EVENTS

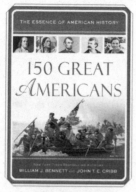

9781400325795

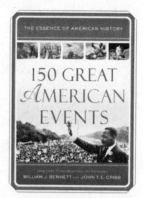

9781400326167

Author and educator William J. Bennett and John T. E. Cribb have a masterful grasp of our history and offer 150 examples of fascinating details of great Americans. This two-volume series is compiled from their bestselling book, *The American Patriot's Almanac*, and has been revised and updated.

150 Great Americans and *150 Great American Events* includes:

- American drama and interesting facts about important American figures
- Obscure details about American history
- Patriotic facts to broaden one's sense of the past
- Bold personalities and internal conflicts
- Discoveries, ideas, and more

Easy-to-read entries and great for history buffs, home-schoolers, teachers, and people who are interested in American history.

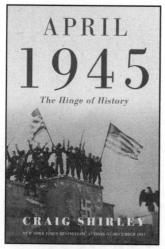

From the Publisher

GREAT BOOKS

ARE EVEN BETTER WHEN THEY'RE SHARED!

Help other readers find this one:

- Post a review at your favorite online bookseller

- Post a picture on a social media account and share why you enjoyed it

- Send a note to a friend who would also love it—or better yet, give them a copy

Thanks for reading!